OTHER BOOKS BY STAN STEINER

The Spirit Woman (1980)
Fusang: The Chinese Who Built America (1979)
In Search of the Jaguar: The Paradox of Development in
    Venezuela (1979)
The Vanishing White Man (1976)
The Islands: The Worlds of the Puerto Ricans (1974)
Borinquen: An Anthology of Puerto Rican Literature,
    editor, with Maria Teresa Babin (1974)
The Tiguas: The Lost Tribe of City Indians (1972)
The Way: An Anthology of American Indian Writing,
    editor, with Shirley Hill Witt (1972)
Aztlan: An Anthology of Mexican-American Literature,
    editor, with Luis Valdez (1972)
La Raza: The Mexican Americans (1970)
George Washington: The Indian Influence (1970)
The New Indians (1968)
The Last Horse (1961)

The
Ranchers

Illustrated by Lloyd Bloom

The Ranchers

A Book of Generations

Stan Steiner

Alfred · A · Knopf   New York   1980

THIS IS A BORZOI BOOK
PUBLISHED BY ALFRED A. KNOPF, INC.

Library of Congress Cataloging in Publication Data
Steiner, Stanley [date]   The ranchers.
1. Ranch life—The West—History. 2. The West
Social life and customs. 3. Ranchers—The West—
Biography. I. Title.
F596.S833   1980   978   80-7646
IBN 0-394-50193-4

Manufactured in the United States of America
First Edition

To Boyd and Anne Charter

CONTENTS

1   The Prologue   I

2   In the Beginning   27

3   The Old Days   51

4   Communities of Rugged Individualists   75

5   In the Sweat of Thy Face Shalt Thou Eat Bread   99

6   Sisters of Ruth and Other Ranch Women   129

7   School Days   155

8   The Children of Eden   177

9   And Thou Art Cursed Above All Cattle   203

10 The Epilogue   233

The Prologue

1

On that clear Montana morning I headed out of town, down the dirt county road along the Rosebud Creek, to visit with an old homesteading family. Though we had never met, we had written to one another, and they knew I was coming. At least I hoped they did. For these folks, the Spragues, had no telephone and no electricity and no way of telling me if they weren't home. And they lived thirty miles from town, on that county road, then five more miles down a rutted ranch road.

Sometimes it seems to me that every homesteading rancher I've ever known lived at least thirty miles out of town, or more. Maybe that's how they have survived this century.

Anyway, I finally found the place, but they weren't home. In front of their log house were two convalescing old cars and a sick tractor. No one else was around but a couple of disdainful horses and a sleeping dog who woke up long enough to bark once or twice without bothering to get up and then went back to sleep.

I sat down under a tree to meditate on my situation, and fell asleep.

On the road, visiting out in ranch country, you get used to that. About half the time when you come visiting, the rancher will be out haying, or working the fences, if you're lucky. Because, if you're not lucky he is likely to have gone to a wedding or funeral in the next county and won't be home for a week.

And so I searched out the nearest neighbor, some five miles

down the road, to ask where the Spragues were. They had gone to a family funeral, in Denver, said the neighbor, but were planning to come back soon because they expected a visitor. Probably me.

In the hope that the neighbor was right, I decided to spend the night in the little farm town of Ashland, which was maybe thirty miles away. Once Ashland was known, to those who knew Ashland, for its Feed Bag Café; but the Feed Bag Café had closed. And so the town was quieter than ever.

That night there was a loud summer cloudburst. And by the next morning the county road had become a thirty-mile-long mud hole. But my car was getting to know the road to the Spragues', even under water.

Driving up to the ranch house, I knew the gods were smiling on me. The Spragues had come home. And so we sat down for a neighborly visit that lasted the morning, drinking coffee by the pot, which they brewed on an old wood cookstove in the log house their pioneering ancestors built. We praised the superiority of the old ways and lamented with a cheerful melancholy the spiritual decline of the rest of America and extolled the moral virtues of living without "store-bought" electricity. By noon we had become more than passing friends.

Now, the Spragues live the way they do by choice. One of their sons works in the electric power plant, at Colstrip, not fifteen miles away, but they "kind of like" not depending on electricity.

I asked why.

"Can't afford electricity," Harold snapped.

But his wife, Virginia, just smiled and said, "Truth is that Harold likes to warm up the rivets in the seat of his old Levi's by the wood fire in the cookstove on a chill morning. Says that it warms his soul."

Harold nodded.

"And you just can't do that properly with one of those electric stoves." He grinned.

Why not, I asked.

"Too impersonal," he said. "It don't feel right. It's sort of a philosophical thing."

"And besides, that wood cookstove, it saves energy," Virginia

Sprague said. "We don't use energy that doesn't come from our own ranch. We get by on 'homemade' energy, you might say, the old way. And the way the cost of energy keeps on going up, maybe soon the old way will be the new way."

The old way will be the new way.

It might seem an irony of history that the descendants of a pioneer family who had come west in search of a better way of life would live without electricity in the shadow of one of the country's biggest power plants. The irony is even greater. Under the buffalo grass on the Sprague ranch, beneath the floorboards of their log house, are millions of tons of coal. And the power companies have offered huge sums of money for the right to strip-mine that coal, to extract its energy for use in the faraway cities.

But the Spragues, like so many of the homestead ranchers, have stubbornly refused to lease or to sell their land. They have obstinately held on to a way of life and a way of thinking that the rest of the country long ago abandoned and forgot. They have grown defiant, in their quiet way.

And why? To preserve a nineteenth-century way of living in the twentieth century? To defend the bygone belief that people should not depend on more than they can make or grow with their own hands, a peculiar philosophy in our consumer society? To keep the faith in a long-gone rural America of communities built upon memories of individual decency and personal honor? To perpetuate a nostalgia for myths about a way of living that may never have existed as it is remembered?

Not that all, or even most, homesteading ranchers live as the Spragues do. They don't. Many have ranching operations as up-to-date as those of computerized feedlots. But, in their minds, the way they see the world and see themselves, they are all of them—Spragues.

Some have said that these old-time ranchers are merely being ornery. And surely they are that. They are iconoclastic, idiosyncratic, individualistic, and hopelessly old-fashioned as well. But that does not tell you, however, why and how they have survived. Everyone knows they should have died out economically years ago.

On the plains and mountains of the high country there are

hundreds of these ranching families, living on the homesteads that their pioneering ancestors built. They go on ranching in old and new ways, hidden in the nooks and crannies, valleys and flats, of the West, where the countryside has barely changed since wagon-train days. And these families are the second, third, fourth, fifth, and sometimes sixth generation on their place. In one place, on the earth, for all that time.

In America, that is a small miracle.

To be able to say, as Mrs. Sprague did, "My roots? I don't have to go looking for my roots. Why, my roots are right here in our house, in our pasture, underfoot in the grass," may seem remarkable. But that is only because so few could say that.

No one had ever asked them how they'd done it, and why. So I decided to ask them, not for the memories of the romantic past, not for quaint stories of rural life to titillate the urban reader, not for "oral history" so academics could use it for their Ph.D.'s, not even for fantasies of the "old days" they had come to believe. And so I decided to ask them simply: Why and how did you survive, and what, if anything, do you think the country can learn from the way you have survived?

In my many years of wanderings through the West I have traveled hundreds of thousands of miles. On the back roads, county roads, ranch roads, abandoned roads, and no roads, I have probably been to, passed through, stopped at, most every small town and ranch crossroads. That may be regarded as an exaggeration, but after more than thirty years of wanderings it doesn't seem like very much of one to me.

One summer when I had begun seriously to work on this book, I started in eastern Oregon, went through northern Nevada, clear across Idaho and Utah into Montana, going north and south, east and west, then down through Wyoming and Colorado, and farther south into the Texas panhandle and New Mexico until I reached the Mexican borderland near the ghost town of Shakespear.

And it was on these roads that I met the ranchers who appear on these pages. They are a cast of characters as singular as they are unique, befitting the sweep and variety of ranch life in the high country.

Now I will introduce them, one by one, as I met them on my odyssey.

The Jordan River flows through eastern Oregon, when it flows, much less dramatically than its famous namesake. But the country seems the same. On the banks of the river the hills look like those of Galilee. Mostly the land is desert, with a sparse covering of wild grasses and scrub and sage. No wonder the pioneer settlers named this place with biblical awe and fear. There was something here that reminded them of the sacrifices and hardships told of in the Old Testament.

Life was hard and only the humblest and the strongest survived. That unusual combination of traits seemed to grow on homestead ranches.

Of all the pioneer families in the Jordan Valley none have been there longer than the Skinners, who had "come across" in the 1860s, even before the old Military Road to Oregon was built. In those days the Indians helped clear their land and were good neighbors; it was that long ago. Bob Skinner, Sr., can still fondly remember where the Indian camps were.

Six generations of Skinners have been born on their ranch. When I visited with them, four generations, I think, were there to welcome me. To some the Skinners may seem a hard and tight-lipped people, but I found them to be much too talkative and their hospitality to be generous and too fattening. That's an occupational hazard in visiting with ranchers—too much hospitality.

Some say Bob Skinner, Jr., resembles Gary Cooper in style. But I found him an eloquent and loquacious man, whether he was talking about the beauty of the leaves in autumn, by the creek, or his old-type corral fences made of packed reeds. Like his father, he is a sentimental realist. Though their ranch house is as modern as their farm equipment, down by the corrals they have reconstructed their old homestead cabin, hauling it for miles over the hills so that it would be nearby.

That homestead cabin is like a beloved gravestone to them, a shrine to their family history. Now that's a case of preserving your roots, with your own hands.

Leaning on the fence, squinting at the sun, his hat pushed back and his blue eyes shining, Bob Skinner said to me as I left, "You know, that old stagecoach road went right by near here. My great-grandfather built that road. If we had to sell out this place I don't know if I could live somewheres else. What if we can't survive? What will we do? Where will we go?"

He smiled. "At night sometimes, you know, I still hear the stage going by."

The generations of pride which a family cherishes in creating their own place on earth may come to a sad and sudden end, but it does not easily die. It lingers on like an echo of hoofbeats, after the rider has vanished over the hills. Up near the Stinking Water Pass, outside the dying town of Drewsey, I met a real old-time rancher who knew that his way of life was dead. "Probably I'm back in the dinosaur age." He laughed. But that didn't change the way he lived one bit.

On the morning we drove up to Glen Sitz's ranch he was out haying. It was a hot, almost unbearable August day, so we sat down under a tree with the buzzing flies to wait until he came home, for lunch, around noon.

Sitz was seventy-three. He lived alone. He worked alone. That summer he had just one "hand," he laughed: his fifteen-year-old granddaughter. In his ranch house, since his wife had died some years ago, things hadn't gone to seed so much as they just fell apart. The roof was leaking. The wallpaper was peeling. The upright piano in the corner was covered with dust.

I asked him why he went on ranching by himself, at his age. And this is what he said. "My father said, 'To be a good buckaroo you had to be smarter than a cow.' And I kinda think that's right.

"We're about the fourth generation here. I guess. Dad come here, and I just kinda fell into it. And I suppose that's the reason I'm here. This here particular country, that's all I know. And I'm a little almost bitter, and of course Republican, about the government coming and trying to tell me how to ranch.

"In the old times and even now it gets ingrained into you to do with what you have. Maybe you call it ingenuity. Or bragging. But you learn to do things with your hands and what brain you might have. I just believe that if you have the ability to work hard and stick to it you can make it."

Fine! Fine! I said. But at your age you can't go on much longer. Why do you do it?

"Why do I work in the fields? Damned if I know. I guess it's a habit. I know maybe I should quit, but I don't want to quit. On some days when I am broken down I just figure there's something wrong in my damned head. If there is a reason why a teacher teaches, or a writer writes, or I stay here on the ranch, it must be because we like it. I guess. And because when you get older you get in a rut. Oh, I don't know any answers."

Sitz is like a man with a terminal disease—his way of life— who has decided to live as fully as a man might. "He is an old-timey, real life, rugged individualistic bastard," said a neighboring rancher. "Not a hell of a lot like him around anymore." Still, he is a small man, lean, unpretentious, and a little shy. And his unassuming way of talking barely hides the fact that his opinions, though pithy, are as sharp as aged whiskey.

"When I die I would like to die quick. And die here. On the ranch," he said.

The loneliest of ranchers, like old Sitz, seem to have that same sense of belonging to a place and of holding onto its memories as do families like the Skinners. No matter how hard they may curse their lonely life and curse ranching itself, they do so with muted pride. They are quiet men—capable of great anger.

Down the road from the Sitz ranch in the crossroads town of Juntura, where the café is, there is such a man. His name is Gerald Allen.

Old bachelor that he is, Gerald Allen has had an unconsummated love and hate affair with ranching. He left his father's "damn ranch" when he was fourteen. And he has done more things and been more places than he "cares to remember." After drinking his way around the country for twenty-five years, he came back to the ranch when his father and brother died.

"Someone had to keep the damned place going," he said. "I couldn't let it die."

The ranch is a monument to the accurate history of cattle

ranching. Homesteaders were first sheep men, then cattle ranchers—"like many ranchers hereabouts was at first. If you look closely at most cattlemen you'll see sheep wool between their teeth. Shit, people look down on sheep men," he cursed, "like they was dirty. Hell, I'm proud of our history."

"Shit shovelers! That's all we cattle ranchers are," he said firmly.

As a bachelor, he spat out his curses like buckshot. There are no women in his house.

In the majestic old ranch house where he lives the rooms are dark, the curtains drawn, the furniture piled high with old newspapers, the kitchen table set with yesterday's dishes. But beneath the disarray of his life he has preserved his family's traditions.

Does that mean he will stay on the ranch now?

"Shit, no!" he burst out. "If it were up to me I won't be here talking to you. If my dad come back, from the grave, and saw the situation that ranching was in he'd throw up his hands, and run."

What will he do?

Allen grinned like a mischievous boy, pulled his "Cat" farm cap down to his eyes and growled, "As a kid I was real contented here. I liked buckarooing. I liked going out to the sheep camps. So I'm going to become a sheepman and to hell with 'em."

Like his father was?

"Now, you can't make a diplomat out of a shit shoveler." He grinned. "It won't work."

As gentle as he is angry, there is a very different sort of homesteading family just across the Idaho line. Marian and Frank Shiveley are a quiet, polite, and kindly old couple.

The little frame house with its green lawn and careful flowers in the suburb of a shopping center near Caldwell, in southwestern Idaho, where they live, is a long way from the rough hills and desert flats of Elko, Nevada, where they ranched for more than half a century. For the Shiveleys are not the descendants of homesteaders; they are homesteaders themselves.

Marian and Frank have now retired from ranching. But behind

their suburban façade they have created a miniature ranch, with a small pasture surrounded by a three-pole fence, a place for a few horses, some fruit trees, a berry patch, and vegetable garden; not to mention the shed where Frank still makes his old-style lariats of braided rawhide. He tans, cleans, cuts, and braids the leather in his old ways.

Where does he sell them?

"Oh, a rodeo cowboy now and then," he says. "Mostly I sell them to dentists from Los Angeles."

He is a wiry, thin, leathery man himself, one of those whose hard life has made him kindhearted and has given him a tolerant humor about human misfortune.

As for Marian, she is that kind of woman who doesn't show her age. She is almost girlish. She may be seventy, or eighty, or ninety. I didn't ask her. The romance of ranch life has not gone from her face. When she remembers the old days on the ranch her eyes are full of delight. The memory of being snowed in for months makes her think of a funny story.

On the summer afternoon when we talked, for six hours, maybe more, in the kitchen, Marian and Frank sat together. They shared their memories as they must have shared their lives. Even in telling of how they "made-do" by turning whiskey bottles into canning jars, Frank had just as much to say as Marian did.

That's something I'd noticed in talking with many old ranching couples: men and women seemed to do a great deal of sharing. Maybe there was less emphasis on "woman's work" and "man's work" when everybody had to work together in order to survive.

All the while we talked Marian held Frank's hand tightly. Occasionally, she would poke him in the forearm with a finger, if he said something that she thought was particularly outlandish.

"Oh, Frank," she would say.

Smiling, he would return her affectionate look. He went on for almost an hour telling how and why he had courted her, enjoying every memory.

It's good to see, I said, that a couple who have lived together for as long as you two have can really still be in love.

"Fifty years," Marian said.

And I get the feeling that you respect each other, I said.

"Respect!" Frank said, as though I had insulted him. "There's no one in this world I respect more. Man can't be in love with his wife if he doesn't respect her."

In some ways the Shiveleys made me think of the Spragues. So many of these old ranching couples had strong marriages that they had built like some edifice, like their ranch house itself, struggling against the elements, against the seasons, against the erosion of time. Their bodily bonds seemed almost biblical, seemed to be strengthened by adversity.

One of these enduring marriages was that of Anne and Boyd Charter. The Charters may have been the best known, and were surely the most outspoken old-time ranchers in Montana, a reputation not uninfluenced by the wide knowledge that Boyd's father had ridden with Butch Cassidy and the Sundance Kid.

Boyd was so conservative he was radical. That is, he was a radical conservative; he left the Republican Party because it had abandoned the policies of Theodore Roosevelt. And he once told me that in his youth there wouldn't have been a Watergate. If a politician lied, we just shot him, he said.

Anne was tough as Boyd was. But her approach to things was more subtle. She grew up in St. Louis, a rich man's daughter who had married a poor cowboy, a beautiful girl who had become a beautiful woman. Her spirit was as unbroken and defiant as his. She was one of those women who decide what they want in life, and get it.

They fought hard all their lives for the way of life they believed in, she by choice, he by inheritance. Boyd was born when the grass was tall, he said, and the land was just as the Indians had left it. "It was beautiful country, more beautiful than you can imagine. The land was as free as the day it was born and created. Every mile of this land, I have known."

And Boyd and Anne tried to keep it that way. They were pioneers in the ranchers' battle against the strip-mining of the range. Outspoken and direct, Boyd was not afraid to tell the state governor what he thought, to his face, curses and all.

The ranch where they lived deep in the Bull Mountains symbolized everything they believed in. It was built as a log house, rough-hewn as Boyd, but it was homey and comfortable, warmed by Anne's wit and intelligence. Proud of the buffalo grass, waist high, that covered the hills, they were prouder still that the land "was just as it was when the first wagon train came through this valley."

In the summer of the writing of this book, when Boyd died, Anne vowed to go on with his fight. She did not have to. Everyone knew she would.

A man who would have liked Boyd was Rex Bundy. They were two of a kind though they had little in common. Once I described Boyd as the kind of man who always had a four-day growth of beard. Rex is more the one-day beard type, and he might not think being called "mean" is a compliment, as Boyd did.

Rex now lives in a quiet, little house in the Bitterroot Valley. So many outsiders have moved there that he calls the place "the suburbs of California." On the road to Missoula there are half a dozen companies that manufacture prefabricated log cabins, "the instant rustic look," Rex curses.

Not that he's a native himself. In his youth he was a wanderer. Born in Dakota, he blew like a tumbleweed into Montana. He was a rodeo cowboy, a ranch hand, drove trucks, and worked on the oil rigs. There isn't much he hasn't done, but he has "survived his life," scarred but unscathed. In good western fashion he can turn the most frightening experiences into funny stories— of which he has the biggest collection since the days when Artemus Ward and Mark Twain turned the tall tale into respectable literature.

All of his bluster is not bluff, however. Rex is genuinely enraged by what is being done to "what's left of the old days by the almighty dollar!" For "pure greed," he says.

To preserve the West as it was in his memory he has become a writer. As though to keep alive on paper what is not being kept alive in life, Rex is a school of western writing unto himself. His conversation about the past, when he isn't cursing the present, is a one-man graduate course in history.

So he remains an unreconstructed cowboy and an incurable

westerner. "Being a westerner is in the blood," he says; "it's like having a terminal disease."

If there is one man who is more ornery than Boyd Charter and more obstreperous than Rex Bundy it is probably Wallace McRae. Personally he prefers the word "perverse."

On the day I drove up to his Montana ranch, the Rocker Six Cattle Company, he was supervising the building of a new ranch house. It was a big house. And he seemed proud of it, but embarrassed nonetheless, as though it was somehow immodest to build so beautiful a place.

"A rancher likes to think he has a Capuchin aura about himself," McRae said. "To see ourselves as fellows who push turds around with our toes and who lay back and act dumb.

"Most of us, well, about the only image we have of ourselves comes from Owen Wister's *The Virginian*. So that is how we try to act."

But it is an act. McRae's building his new ranch house was his way of telling the coal company that was strip-mining the hills up the road that he was not going to move, sell out, or be bulldozed off his land. He had been defying them for years. He was as humble about it as a shotgun.

His grandfather had homesteaded the family ranch on Rosebud Creek nearly a hundred years ago. The first winter he almost froze to death in a blizzard. "Perverse! We have always been that way I guess," McRae said. "I see that strip mine as just another blizzard."

The land was a member of his family, to McRae. And he has written of it lovingly in the book of poems that he has published, *It's Just Grass and Water*. One poem that seems to voice powerfully his outrage is simply titled "The Land":

> Gestating in the mid-year
> Seldom did it show.
> Youthful green in springtime.
> White and gaunt with snow.
>
> She who each year faithfully
> Gives her produce away,

Never asking compensation.
Quiet, unassuming is her way.

You'd ravish her with mindless lust,
Then curse her for a whore.
You've never loved her as I have
Or you'd respect her more.

Rip open her hard belly.
Tear her vitals out.
Sew her back with zippered tracks
That wander roundabout.

You'd prostitute her beauty
With cosmetic care.
Strip her of fertility
And leave her prostrate there.

In spirit, if nothing more, the feminine equivalent to Wally McRae may be Ellen Cotton, who ranches near Decker, Montana, down near the Wyoming line. For years she has fought off the power companies whose strip mines all but surround her ranch. If they come again, she says, she will go get her shotgun.

Ellen Cotton is a small, demure-looking woman who ranches all by herself. She lives alone, and she can be ornery.

The road to her ranch was rough. No one came out to greet me, and I had the feeling I was being watched. In a corral the horses stirred nervously. And so I drove around the corral and headed into the hills, when I saw the dust of a pickup behind me. A white-haired woman was driving and yelling, "Where the heck you think you are going?"

It was Ellen Cotton. She seemed hostile, her eyes narrowed, her mouth set. When she recognized me her eyes and mouth relaxed. But not much. "Thought you were one of those darned coal company men," she said.

Always greet visitors that way? I asked.

"I can be ornery." She smiled, obviously pleased with herself. "I suppose I don't always mean to be ornery. But I can be."

Can be? I said.

An old woman living alone on an isolated ranch, forty miles from town, she had reason to be suspicious of strangers. She had been threatened. The nearest neighbor was miles away.

She was from New England, of Puritan stock. An old family, from Concord, Massachusetts, near the bridge where the American Revolution began, she said. And she didn't like being pushed around; it was un-American.

And was that why she stayed on an old-fashioned ranch, as if out of spite? I asked.

No, she answered. "In some ways the woman may feel more strongly about it [her ranch] than a man. The man, he may want to move on. But a woman won't. Maybe that's why women do make good ranchers.

"Many of these young women want to make me into a feminist heroine. Because I ranch alone. Because I live like this. That's bullshit! That's ridiculous! That isn't what I want to be. I just like to work with critters.

"I love critters. Gosh. That's why I came out to this country —for God's sake. That's one of the joys of my life.

"And I love ranching the way I do it. My own way."

The folksy and spicy speech of Ellen Cotton and her pioneer philosophy reflect her ranching operation. She might as well be living on the old frontier. She would have liked that, she said.

But then, her family homesteaded long ago back east in Massachusetts. And she is pioneering on a homestead right now, in the West.

One of the older and more settled homesteading families whom I met was that of the Cheneys. They were a "wagon-train family," now in their fifth generation, I believe. When they had come across and settled in the Madison River Valley, north of the Yellowstone, they were among the first white people in the region and their neighbors were mostly Indians.

So they had been there a long time on their homestead. Their ranch had the look of stability and permanence, as though it belonged just where it was. And the ranch house, though modest, was well built and felt comfortable and lived-in. History shadowed its rooms. Roberta Cheney, who showed me around, pointed to a painting by Charles Russell on the living room wall. "That cowboy there," she said of one of the figures in the canvas, "he was my uncle."

The peaceful and beautiful valley where the ranch was located did not appear to have changed much since those days. It was true the fishermen and hunters did disturb its quiet, not to mention the animals, more than before. But old Virginia City, of vigilante fame, lies not far away, so the valley was accustomed to unnecessary disturbances. For all that, there was a serenity in the valley and in the ranch house and in Roberta Cheney.

She had left the valley as a girl and for fifty years had lived in the academic world, as a student and as a teacher. Now she had returned to the ranch with her husband, surrounded that summer by her children and their children. She had retired from the world outside and had come home.

Why did you come back? I asked.

"There are cycles in life, I believe," she said softly, "and I think this completes a cycle of my life. And besides, our children love the ranch and they wished for us to stay here."

And the feeling that their families were as much a part of their ranches as the trees and grasses pervaded the memories of many pioneer homesteaders; a sense that the generations who had lived there were like the cycle of the seasons. They belonged to the ranches as much as their ranches belonged to them. It was a feeling that seemed to come with homesteading.

Of all the ranchers I met none expressed this sense of the land more strongly than Elliott and Omar Barker. For the Barkers it was not an ancestral memory; the brothers had come from Texas, back in 1889, in their family wagon train.

And they remembered it, even now, as though it were yesterday. The trek up the Canadian River, through the old Matador Ranch into the high country of the Pecos, New Mexico, where they had settled. Modestly, but boasting a little, Omar said, "Not a great many people living today can look back on such an experience as a five-hundred-mile migration of covered wagons."

Pa "just hitched up the wagons," Omar recalled, and "struck out to look for some mountains." Just as simple as that.

That's known as telling a tall tale by understating it. But then Omar had become a writer. Some say that he is probably "the dean" of western writers. In his mid-nineties, he is certainly the oldest.

Elliott, the younger brother (he's ninety-three), became known as "Mr. Conservation." A rancher who was a conservationist in the days of Teddy Roosevelt, he has written some of the fundamental conservation acts. But I have always thought he was proudest, or at least most pleased, with having discovered, as he says, Smokey the Bear.

He led pack trains into his late seventies. And he finally gave up horseback riding as reluctantly as some men give up sex.

Maybe the Barker boys are not as spry as they once were. But their activity tires younger men, like me. Last summer Elliott and I teamed up at the Western Writers' convention, up in Colorado. Elliott had asked me to drive him up because the State Highway Department refused to let him operate a car anymore. Once at the convention he regaled the audience with ranching tall tales.

One of his favorite lines was in response to the question, How did a man like you, who as a pioneer conservationist had so many enemies, overcome them all?

"That's easy," he said, "I outlived them."

As good a teller of understated New Mexican tall tales, all of them true, is William Lumpkin. His folks ranched in Lincoln County, New Mexico, during the Billy the Kid years, all the qualification that a man might need.

Lumpkin is a soft-spoken storyteller. His kerchief, his cowboy hat, his full white mustache, make him look like the stereotype of the old-time rancher. But he isn't.

The old family ranch was in Lincoln County, but his father ran cattle as well on a 250,000-acre spread near the Apache high country of Arizona until he lost that ranch back in the 1920s. One uncle was a foreman on the famed Matador Ranch and another was a judge during the Lincoln County War, if I remember rightly. And it seems the Lumpkins have always been embattled; no less than ten Lumpkins were with Washington at Valley Forge, all of them Kentucky long-riflemen.

"Old Joseph Lumpkin, who was my great-great-grandfather, and his nine sons, were almost an army in themselves," Lumpkin says.

Still, for all that, my old friend Bill Lumpkin is a quiet, unassuming, and gentle man. He wears his heritage with grace. And he himself is an architect and artist, maybe one of the best-known adobe architects in the Southwest. It's just that he tells old-time ranching stories of youth so well, and expresses the homestead philosophy so strongly.

Mostly it's the old style of storytelling that Lumpkin symbolizes. Listen to this: "On the ranch we had a foreman who was so bowlegged that a hog could run between his legs and not scratch him," Bill began a story. "He got killed in a stampede during a lightning storm. He tried to turn the cattle, but he didn't make it. Evidently his horse stumbled or something. There were only pieces of him left."

And with a grin, Bill nodded. "A cowboy's life wasn't easy."

Not too far up the road from the old Lumpkin place, just over the mountains, is the ranch of Billy Stephenson. He is a young man and lives very much in the present, not the past. If the legends of Billy the Kid have crossed his pasture, he pays them no mind; he's more interested in his cows.

And Stephenson is trying to hold onto his ranch, by grit and ingenuity. His land is threatened not by history, but by developers.

The ranch lies east of the Capitan Mountains, a mountain range so majestic the developers have already sold the far side to vacationers. "More profitable to raise skiers than cows," Stephenson said. "In this high desert you need one hundred acres for a cow. Maybe more. And those vacation homes, they're lucky if they got a whole acre.

"In a way the subdividers are like coyotes," he said. "Just waiting till some rancher gets weak enough so they can go and jump in for a killing. Ranchers are being mostly crowded out by outsiders. The price of land is so high that another rancher can't buy a place that's for sale. They go to some absentee owner who couldn't care less about the land.

"Ranchers are fewer in number all the time," Stephenson said. "Do we have to get to the point where there's hardly any ranches left before they start seriously thinking about that down in Washington? I don't know."

Even so, the Stephenson ranch, the I–X, seems to be set down on the earth as solidly as a rock. The huge trees that shade the ranch house appear generations old. And the ranch house itself, built around the original log cabin which is now the kitchen, has been made modestly luxurious by the carpentry of Stephenson's own hands.

The barns and outbuildings are trim, in spite of Stephenson's not being able to hire more than one hand, to help him with the work.

"If we go under it won't be for want of hard work," he said. "And I sure don't intend to go under. Not without a fight."

Deeper in the desert, farther to the south, down near the Mexican border just outside of Lordsburg, New Mexico, are two ranchers who are just as determined to hold onto the old virtues of ranching philosophy. They are mother and daughter, Rita and Janaloo Hill, of Shakespear.

The ranch of these two women is headquartered in the ghost town of Shakespear, which they own. They live in the old general store, a barnlike building full of mementos and relics of the frontier West when the stagecoach stopped right here. On the porch is one of the stagecoaches that made the run up to Silver City.

Shakespear is that kind of place. They say that John Ringo lived here once, and Billy the Kid washed dishes and waited tables in the café.

Rita Hill came here long ago—she wouldn't say when. Her husband was the last "real cowboy" in the territory, she said. But there are those who would say that that honor ought to go to Rita Hill herself.

She is a small woman, lean as she is tough. In preserving their ranch she has fought the state and federal governments single-handedly, halting an interstate highway across her land for almost a year.

Politely, at first, Mrs. Hill protested when the highway engineers decided to build an interchange in the middle of one of her best pastures. "My cows don't need a highway interchange," she told them. They would not listen to her. And so she erected a one-room shack in the path of the highway and moved in. For a year she defied the efforts of the state and federal governments to force her out.

"In preserving our ranch we were preserving the history of the American West," said daughter Janaloo. "This ranch is living history." And Janaloo, who takes care of the cattle, is in fact the unofficial historian of Shakespear.

I asked her why she didn't write that history down.

"Too busy taking care of the cows," she said.

That, come to think of it, is what ranching is all about. Cows! It is strange that the feeding and care of so prosaic an animal should breed so many heroic legends, and historic myths, and spirited people.

Consider the Pettits.

In some ways Ruth and Tug Pettit epitomize the breed of pioneers who have been forever movin' on and settlin' down and movin' on again, taking the spirit of America along with them, re-creating it, because for them the frontier could never die; it lived in their lives, their thoughts, their way of talking.

Pettits had come into Texas in the 1830s or 1840s from Alabama. They had homesteaded, at first, in Comanche County, and later up near Canyon City, not far from the old Goodnight spread, and then near Lubbock, and later still in South Texas, before the dust storms of the 1930s blew them out of the state of Texas entirely.

That was when Ruth and Tug decided to go on what they called "the last wagon train west" in 1932. Poor and just about done in, they fitted out two of their farm wagons with a canvas top, and drove what little was left of their herd, about eighty head, through the deserts and over the Sacramento Mountains, in the wilderness, away from the roads, for 450 miles into New Mexico; a journey of three months.

Once settled, the Pettits homesteaded again. Their homesteading was in some ways even more courageous than their journey.

Each time, in each place and generation they settled, they had to begin all over again. As though they were literally carrying a movable frontier along with them.

Ruth said, "When I think of coming across in that covered wagon, I tell you, I wouldn't do it again."

"I would," said Tug.

Now that they were in their seventies, I asked them, were they ready at last to settle down and get out of the ranching business?

"Well, no," Tug said, grinning mischievously, "never been completely out of ranching. Never will be. Now we run a ranch in California. Though I ride out just once a week. In a jeep."

Fittingly, I think, my visit with the Pettits took place in a mobile home owned by their son high in the Sangre de Cristo (Blood of Christ) Mountains, of New Mexico.

The mobile home was parked in the forest near the end of the Old Santa Fe Trail.

Now these ranchers were not the only ones whom I visited with and whose words I have gathered.

In some ways they do seem to be a pretty good cross section of some of the men and women on homestead ranches. That's about all they really have in common. Most of them are the descendants of homesteaders, or are homesteaders themselves. As one rancher told me: Every hill and gully is different from any other hill and gully.

Never have I met a typical rancher and I hope I never will. I doubt that such an animal exists. Besides, it wouldn't be fitting for folks who pride themselves on being independent-minded to be considered typical of anyone but themselves.

In any event, this is not a Gallup poll, nor a sociological study, nor a statistical survey of ranchers and ranching. This is an appreciation of a way of life, a homage, a requiem and a celebration, an invocation of the spirit.

Some of these ranchers are old friends I have known for years. Some I had never met before. Some were introduced to me by mutual acquaintances. Some I got to know through ranching and cattlemen's groups. Some I met by chance along the roadside, in cafés and in bars.

None of them were chosen because of their philosophy, but rather because of how well they expressed it, no matter what that philosophy was.

In a sense they selected themselves. They are the people who were the most articulate, the most outspoken, and the most able to voice what they felt.

And I simply listened and tried not to ask too many questions. One does not interview ranchers, one visits with them.

One thing I learned in talking to ranchers: you have to let the men and women speak their own piece and do so in their own good time. Most ranchers on being asked about this or that would respond, at first, by saying, "Reckon I don't rightly have much to say about that." And then, if given half the chance, would talk nonstop for hours.

Ranchers, like most rural people I know, like to talk. "It beats workin'," one fellow said when I complained that he had been talking for five hours and I was tired of listening: listening is sometimes more tiring than talking. Anyway, this fellow had come in from haying and so I asked him if he didn't have to finish his haying. "Hell, that hay ain't going nowheres." He smiled and went on with his tale of how on that day in 1916 when . . .

The ranchers' way of talking comes from an old storytelling tradition. In the days before radio and television, when a man or woman told a story sitting on a porch, or leaning on a fence, the telling would go on for hours, or at least until that story was finished. It was not a world tuned in to the thirty-second commercial.

And ranchers still like to tell a story that way. It is a way the native Americans like, as well.

Many of the ranchers eagerly welcomed the opportunity to have their say. They felt no one listened to their admonitions and thoughts, and when they talked, what they said was usually distorted by the urban provincialism of the press and the government.

And when I offered them not merely a sympathetic ear, but an entire book, in which to speak their piece, the words poured forth. The image of the laconic, tight-lipped, and taciturn ranchers popularized by Gary Cooper and John Wayne quickly disappeared.

Even worse were ranchers who began by saying, "Now, I don't have much of what you call education." That, I found out, was a way of saying that they didn't think highly of "educated" men; it was a critical and angry statement clothed in politeness, and the rancher who said it was about to unleash a verbal attack on just about everything in sight.

In this there is a style of talking that I have come to call "immodest modesty." Saying things in such a way that the most powerful opinion seems to be offered humbly, almost with an apology; it is a rural style that is as deceptive as it is disarming. Though that is not, I think, its purpose.

More likely it is a kind of safety valve, a way for the speaker to protect himself from any wrath of the gods that he may have evoked by speaking out. Those people who are close to the earth often seem to feel that way.

And it is a style of talk that recognizes that nature is more powerful than anything a human may say—no matter how powerfully. So having cursed the heavens and the earth, the rancher steps back, not so much in humility as in the knowledge that the heavens, and the earth, will have the last word anyway.

That sense of human vulnerability was best conveyed by Frank Shiveley the day I visited with him and his wife. For hours, as we sat in the kitchen, he went on and on with one story after another about the old days. Each one was better than the one before, longer, taller, funnier, and more unbelievably true.

Marian finally kicked him affectionately, under the table.

"Oh, Frank!" she said, exasperated, and she chided him: "You tell them storics so often that you are beginning to believe them."

Frank leaned back, balancing his chair on two legs, in midair, the way storytellers do, and he tipped his cowboy hat back, and squinted happily at his wife.

"Nope," he grinned, "I only half believe them."

In the Beginning

2

We Were the Last Known Wagon Train
Tug and Ruth Pettit

There's some tell us that we were the last known wagon train to come across from Texas.

And that was in 1932.

Four hundred and fifty miles. And three months and nine days coming across. We rigged up some farm wagons like covered wagons. We had our vaqueros up ahead and we brought eighty-seven head of cattle up behind the wagons. And that way we come across the plains and on through the mountains and deserts.

We come by covered wagon, yes, sir, we come by covered wagon. We surely did.

Come right down the Penasco River, off the Pecos. And we crossed the Sacramento Mountains. And we didn't go through the Dog Canyon either. And we crossed the White Sands desert. And we had a time of it. Some places we couldn't get the wagons down off the mesas.

And when we got down where the water was, they were trying to kill off the wild horses and burros. So they had cut off the water. They just left one big tub with water and they had a guy posted there with a Winchester rifle. If you tried to get water there, he'd shoot you down. That was drought time.

And they would call a guy from El Paso. He'd come up and pick up the body. For three cents a pound.

Well, when we got into that country we didn't have no water.

So we had to go break a water line. The water spurted twenty feet high. We like drowned.

Up there in the mountains we broke a wagon axle. And so we had to build one. We cut down a tree and we hewed it out. We had to get one strong and long enough. 'Course, I done wagon work back home in the shop. And we fit the wheels to it and everything and loaded up the wagon and took off.

And we had to keep the horses from eating the sleeping grass and going off to sleep. Our old mare died out there on the flats.

We had an idea of where we were going. Two of the guys who was with us used to work for those ranchers in there. They knew the way, pretty well.

The ranchers was good to us all the way across; they would send a rider out to see that everything was all right. Well, some looked at us like we was a little bit crazy.

Our folks come out of Alabama maybe around the 1840s. They settled in Comanche County, in Texas. In the 1890s some of them moved out around Lubbock and Canyon, Texas, until some oil fellow swindled my dad out of most of his land. So, after a while, we went south to a ranch, but the drought and the grasshoppers wiped us out.

And we decided to come across by covered wagon from Texas. We was going west, alooking for a home.

We left the bears some tracks.

Remembering that last wagon train to the West, not into the wilderness, but away from the dust bowl of the Great Depression, traveling through the backcountry to stay off the highways, not to escape from Indians but from small-town sheriffs who often turned back migrating Okies, both Ruth and Tug Pettit breathed a sigh of remembered relief. And became suddenly silent.

Then Ruth said, "When I think of coming across in that covered wagon, I tell you, I wouldn't do it again."

"I would," said Tug.

One thing about this modern-day bit of pioneering struck

me at once: the last wagon train of the Pettit family coming out of Texas, in 1932, was remarkably like the first wagon train of the Pettit family coming into Texas, in 1830, or was it in 1840? Much had changed, of course, but it hadn't changed all that much.

In the plains and mountains of southeastern New Mexico the range was largely unfenced, until the mid-1930s. So it was still open range.

And the hardships on the trail, the broken wagon axle, the dry, hot desert, the armed guard at the lone water hole, could just as well have been one hundred years ago, in time and in place. Most of all, the spirit and the endurance of these latter-day pioneers resembled that of their early ancestors.

"Sure," Tug said, "my folks always been doing what they should've known better than have done."

From their childhood, in a way, Ruth and Tug Pettit had been prepared for the day they would become pioneers once more. Their memory of youth spent on their parents' homesteads made that clear.

And We Didn't Have No House to Live In
Tug and Ruth Pettit

RUTH: The old ranch house is still standing in Comanche County, Texas. It is still livable. It is put together with pegs and no nails at all.

TUG: It's about three feet off of the ground. Was on the ground, but now the ground's eroded. And we left there in the winter of 1899. Come up to Lubbock, Texas, and my dad homesteaded that place and then he bought several homesteaders out.

RUTH: Tug, he was just a yearling, then. He was just one year old.

TUG: And we didn't have no house to live in. We camped in the wagons. We had two wagons. They used to call that a "fly-out-over-the-chuckbox." And we used to sleep that way until dad went one hundred and ten miles to town to get us some lumber.

Then we dug a dugout. What they'd call a half-dugout. We dug it down just so deep and then we made a roof over it and covered it with dirt. Then we fared pretty well.

Come the snow, well, it got pretty well covered. That was tough.

And I remember we would bed out, you know, when I had to stand guard with the cattle. And it would be as nice as it is now. And we would take naps in relay. And you'd wake up the next morning and there would be snow on top of your bed. One thing was to get out in all that snow and get out to the chuck wagon. Sure was cold.

RUTH: On the plains I guess you do know what we used for firewood. There were no sage. There were no trees. So they used buffalo chips, first. And when I was young they used plain old cow chips. In the fall you'd take the wagon, and all the kids, and neighbors they'd be doing the same thing, and you'd pick up cow chips and pile them up and gather them in the wagon and bring them in.

TUG: And one winter we had these sacks of maize and corn-cobs, and we couldn't sell them for anything. So that's what we used for firewood. Corncobs sure make a nice hot fire. And the maize, that would pop like popcorn, but not as big as a popcorn. But we ate that stuff.

In those days we sure had to do everything the hard way. Not just was it a hundred and ten miles to town, but if you went anywhere it was on horseback, or by a buggy. There were no cars.

Growing up? Was it fun growing up? I don't know how we stood it!

Few people do personally remember coming west in a covered wagon. And those few grow fewer every year. Those who remember the memories of others, of parents and grandparents and great-grandparents, are greater in number. For, as Omar Barker has forlornly said of the survivors, "Not a great many people living today can look back on such an experience as a five-hundred-mile migration of covered wagons."

He can. He came that way. He remembers every day of that trip.

When Barker was a young man he became not a cowpuncher, but a "typewriter puncher," as he says, because there was no land left for him on the family ranch. But he was "ranch bred." A modest man, his gentle face belied his shrewd and knowing eyes that had seen almost one century of ranching history.

Still, it is not history to him. It is simply the story of his family.

Maybe he would agree with old J. M. Shiveley who had advised covered-wagon pioneers, in 1846: "When the emigrants start they should not fancy that they are doing some great thing." They will not need any "military array, &c, all that is folly," he said; a covered wagon train is a family affair, like any other, with all the problems of family living, and then some.

And that's how Omar Barker described it, too.

One Day Dad Just Hitched Up the Wagons
Omar S. Barker

About the Barker family's trek from Texas to New Mexico, in 1889, Pa used to like to say that he just hitched up the wagons one morning, rounded up the livestock, whistled for the dogs, hollered for the young 'uns, and struck out to look for some mountains. There was some truth in this, because both Squire Leander Barker and Priscilla Jane McGuire Barker were Blue Ridge Mountain born and never had been very happy in the mid-Texas lowlands.

But there was more to it than that—drought and hard times for one thing.

For four years drought had made all that part of Texas a land of bitter poverty and near-starvation. The Farmers' Alliance even sent Pa to Dallas and Fort Worth to beg help wherever he could. He came back with three carloads of food and clothing for the destitute people of the area. Though prosperous enough now, Shackelford County didn't look then like much of a place to raise a family.

There was also the fact that we all ailed a good deal from

chills and fever, but the real big reason for the move was that Ma suffered from asthma, which we hoped a change of climate might cure.

So he sold the place on Battle Creek for whatever he could get, and on the morning of August 22, 1889, the Barkers hitched up and headed out northwestward to look for those mountains —and for a new home. While actually there was no great danger involved, it did require some fortitude, especially on my mother's part, to undertake such a trip. As for me, at age eleven, I rode the whole five hundred miles in an old flat-cantled "Texas apple-horn," helping my older brother Ben drive the loose cattle and horses. . . .

Pa drove one covered wagon with a team of oxen named Spot and Coaly, sometimes riding, sometimes walking, beside the steers which he controlled entirely by gees and haws. Incidentally, Pa had some local fame as a driver of oxen because he had taught Spot and Coaly the unheard-of feat of trotting with a wagon.

Ma drove the two-horse team of the second wagon, with Grace, the six-week-old baby, in a crib handily near the seat.

Sixteen-year-old Ida was head driver of the third wagon, with Minnie, fourteen, taking her turn at the reins on either wagon from time to time. The little ones—Pearl, Mattie, and Elliott —rode in whatever wagon came handiest.

The oldest of us, Ben and I, drove the fifty-six cattle and sixteen horses. In only one day the loose horses had begun to learn to follow the wagons, and the cattle to follow the horses. Though there was some longhorn blood in most of them, they were not wild cattle. We tied up the calves of a couple of the best milkers so we could milk the cows in the morning, and bedded the bunch down without any trouble not far from camp. But just to make sure they didn't wander, Ben and I stayed out to guard them and the horses until I got so sleepy I couldn't stay in the saddle, and then Ben guarded them alone well into the night.

The wagons were too full of household goods—a stove, farm and blacksmithing tools, and simple eatables, including a barrel of sorghum for sweetenin'—to leave any room for beds; so except for Ma and the baby we all slept on the ground, in defiance of rattlesnakes, tarantulas, centipedes, and vinegaroons.

The country was full of rattlers, tarantulas, centipedes, and vinegaroons. At a camp on the Clear Fork of the Brazos, near a prairie-dog town, something startled the cattle and as I rode to head them my mare stepped on a rattlesnake. I don't know which was scared worse, me or the mare, but luckily neither of us got bit. That night we could hear the spine-chilling "zzz zzz zzz" of rattlers out in the dark, and Pa had the kids stretch a rope all the way around camp. Whether that kept them out or not, I don't know, but no snakes got into our beds.

Mostly, the country we traveled was unfenced, and we camped wherever water and grass made it convenient. But one evening a man with a six-shooter at his hip rode into camp and informed us that we were trespassing on the famous Matador Ranch, and he sternly ordered us to load up and git, as they didn't propose to have any damned immigrants eating Matador beef.

"Suppose you just look us over, my good Christian friend," Pa told him, "and tell me which one of this outfit looks to you like a thief!"

After some palaver, the man finally agreed to let us camp. I believe Ma invited him to stay for supper, but he didn't accept.

Dropping off the Staked Plain into the breaks south of the Canadian River, we crossed into New Mexico at Glenrio and soon sighted Tucumcari Mountain, named for its resemblance to a woman's figure. Though not as high as those we were soon to see looming up against the western sky, this was the first real mountain any of us kids had ever seen and you may well believe it was quite a thrill. Passing north of it we dropped into the canyon of the Canadian River, passed old Fort Bascom, then already abandoned, and followed up the Canadian on the rough but already ancient route used by the Spanish *ciboleros* and *commancheros* of the Las Vegas country going to the plains to hunt buffalo or trade with the Comanches.

At San Hilario, now vanished deep under the waters of Conchas Dam, we saw our first native village with strings of bright red chili hung out to dry against its brown adobe walls. The fact that none of us knew a word of Spanish and that our old Holstein had whipped some of their bulls didn't keep the natives from being friendly.

The road up Olquin Hill out of the Canadian drainage onto the wide open mesa east of Las Vegas was narrow, rocky, and so steep that Pa had to double-team each wagon to drag them up it. It was the hardest going we had run into, but once we topped the mesa rim, what a sight!

Pa stood a long time looking at it while the tired teams rested. He didn't say much and neither did Ma, but the shine in their eyes was something to see.

From the Bible and the old hymn, "Sweet Beulah Land," Ma named the place "Beulah," the promised land, where she and Pa were content to live the rest of their lives and where they now lie buried under the whispering pines they both loved so well.

Settlers were said to be soldiers in "God's battle" to make the West "His crowning work" on earth, proclaimed Marvels of the West, *written in 1888. Their homesteads were part of a "Divine Plan." And they were fulfilling the commands of "an all wise and over-ruling Providence" by merely going west, declared* The Emigrants' Guide, *written in 1845. For the West was heaven on earth; its scenery was nothing less than "Providence illustrated."*

Not so, said the later historians of the West. To Bernard De Voto, in his chronicle of the frontier, the West was "a country that grew increasingly to look like Hell"; where the sun was "violent," the weather "vicious," the men "gaunt as their stock," and the covered wagons "wrecked."

As always, people who wrote about covered-wagon trains and people who rode the covered-wagon trains, did not see eye to eye, any more than did people who wrote about settlers, and the settlers themselves. They were, as we would say today, on different trips.

To the settlers the West was neither heaven nor hell. It was home.

So Virginia and Harold Sprague remembered their homesteading ancestors as they sat in their ancestors' homestead in Montana. They remembered them as ordinary people who did extraordinary things.

Our Folks, They Pioneered This Country
Virginia and Harold Sprague

VIRGINIA: Our folks, they pioneered this country.

HAROLD: My great-grandfather, he was probably a hunter for the railroad. Both his feet been frozen off. And there was lots of things he couldn't do. But he could ride and shoot. I don't know for sure when he came in, but the railroad came to Miles City in 1881 and he was already here when his family came in 1882. So he came before that.

And I had another grandfather on my mother's side that was crippled in the war. The Civil War. He had an arm that was crippled and the doctors wanted to cut it off. But he wouldn't let them. One of his buddies put a pistol under his bed covers, for him, and he told the doctors he wouldn't let them cut it off.

Anyhow, they came and settled here, and built up a ranch, and made it their life.

Came up Rosebud Creek, where they settled first. They were there, oh, seven years, and then they moved to where there is the Cheyenne Reservation now. The Indian Agency had a bunch of soldiers here. So that was one reason they came here. And the main reason was there was a sawmill and they worked in the mill. But Dad, he had this horse camp here and he homesteaded.

Renegades, what they called them. A bunch of critters and that kinda stuff. This fellow said: I will sell them for what you got in your pocket! And that's how come Dad built this ranch up. This was Dad's homestead. And it burnt down. And he went up to Grandmother's place, up above here where the horse camp was, and took the logs to build this place. Grandmother, she homesteaded it first, it was her logs.

VIRGINIA: There's a sentimental value here, you see.

HAROLD: And these logs, in our place, they've been my grand-mother's and my father's, before us.

VIRGINIA: I been interested in "roots" way before I ever heard of that movie. 'Course, we didn't see it, being without television, but we happened to be at our son's place one night and we just saw one part of it.

And it was interesting.

One thing that these ranchers had in common before they became homesteaders was that few of them had ever been ranchers before. Few of them knew anything about ranching until they came west. They came from the moors of Scotland and Cornwall, from the Isle of Man and Ireland, from the Pyrenees and the Alps and even farther away, from the clerks' desks of Boston and Cincinnati and from the plantations and farms of Atlanta and Montgomery.

And few, if any, of them knew a damn thing about longhorn cattle.

Most of what the emigrants learned about ranching, horseback riding and cattle-raising, roundups and herding, and living alone and making-do in the wilderness, the Indian and Mexican vaqueros, or cowboys, taught them. But that's another story, for another time.

They learned to be ranchers. They became part of the land. And the land became part of them.

On the Skinner Ranch in the Jordan Valley of eastern Oregon, the grandfather of the family, Bob Skinner, Sr., and the father, Bob Skinner, Jr., talked to me of how their forefather came to breed "fancy horses" on the frontier of Nevada, and almost by accident founded their family ranch, unto the sixth generation.

My Great-Grandfather Wasn't a Rancher to Begin With
Robert Skinner, Jr., and Robert Skinner, Sr.

FATHER (Skinner, Jr.): My great-grandfather came from the Isle of Man. He wasn't a rancher to begin with. He built the road, the first road, from the Oregon Trail, on the Owyhee River, to Silver City. It was a toll road. Later he branched out into raising horses, fancy trotting horses. And that required a ranch to take care of the horses. Probably that is one reason he got into ranching and he started this ranch here, in 1878. Ever since then there have been Skinners here.

My great-grandfather, when he acquired this ranch, he traded that toll road and the gate station and his bull team for the land. On the road he had a franchise whereby he could charge so much per head and per wagon.

GRANDFATHER (Skinner, Sr.) : It was a franchise from the territorial government, before this was a state. And we got copies of the paper where the franchise was granted to him.

FATHER: And he traded all of his holdings on the upper part of the Jordan Creek for this place. His old ranch was about a mile and a half from where this ranch headquarters is.

GRANDFATHER: In 1884, his health failed and the family moved to California. And he came back and he operated their holdings up the creek here, about six miles, with a partner.

On the road here was a stagecoach that left every day for Silver City. And a stagecoach that left for Winnemucca, Nevada. And, in those days, our nearest neighbor was three miles away on the Ruby Ranch. And there was a few people living down on the creek. But not many.

FATHER: In those days what was the ranch like? Before the Indians scrubbed off the sagebrush?

GRANDFATHER: Desert. All of this land here, away from the creek, was desert. The best land on the ranch was just the overflow from the creek.

FATHER: What did the countryside look like besides being a piece of ground with a fence around it? Was it sage? Was it grassland?

GRANDFATHER: All the flatland was sagebrush. There was dry grass, tall, native grass. Some.

FATHER: I remember Grandfather saying if you want a good piece of ground to farm, go where the sagebrush grows the tallest.

GRANDFATHER: When I remember this ranch, first the small building over by the river where the family used to live was still standing. My dad, he put up the big house.

FATHER: One of the oldest original buildings wasn't originally here. But we brought it here. The homestead—we call it. It's in terrible shape, but we wanted it here, near the house. So we brought it here and set it up, by the corral.

GRANDFATHER: Yes, sir, my grandfather came here in 1878. To this place. To this very place.

FATHER: And my grandchildren will be the sixth generation.

The upright piano stood in the corner of the parlor where it always had. On the walls around it were old photographs of parents and grandparents, of the early homesteads and favored horses. And though the little ranch house had all the modern appliances and conveniences, these gadgets of consumer technology were surrounded by the heritage of history.

One of the things that Wally McRae took pride in on his Rocker Six Ranch was the meaning of his family traditions.

But that was not unusual. No matter how modest or modern, most ranch houses combined the old and the new. That was the way the ranchers liked to live, with their forebears looking over their shoulders, and watching them closely.

McRae was building a new, large ranch house. And when it was finished you may be sure that the old upright piano would once more be in the parlor, surrounded by the old photographs of all of his homesteading ancestors. "It's not a matter of nostalgia," he would say, "but of preserving and cherishing the spiritual strengths of the old days."

Maybe I'm Just Perverse, the Way My Grandfather Was
Wallace McRae

My grandfather was perverse. Being perverse is a little like being courageous, I suppose. Or dumb.

And the old man, my grandfather, he came from Scotland. Came to Texas. Then came to Montana and worked here on several ranches. He put enough money together where he could buy a bunch of sheep. And he just got this investment in his sheep all made when here came the winter of 1886 and 1887.

Old John McRae, when he came here, I am not sure, but I speculate, he was the victim of an agricultural breakthrough in Scotland. His family were crofters, that is sharecroppers, who

in Scotland ran sheep. And some geneticist had come through with a new brand of sheep that could graze on peat bogs without getting foot rot, opening up all kinds of forage for sheep. And completely ruining the sheep market. The crofters were out. So my grandfather was a victim of that and he came to America.

But he wasn't going to be run out once more. Not by any winter snow.

Someone, a friend of his, who was in town, finally became concerned about him and rented a couple of horses at the livery stable and went out to look for him. He found him plowing around in the snowdrifts. Looking after his sheep in those blizzards.

And so his friend told him: Look, John, I brought this horse out for you to ride back to town.

And the old man, my grandfather, he said, I'm not going back to town. I got these sheep to look after.

And his friend said, John, half of them are dead already. And the rest will be dead by spring and you'll be dead with them. You got to leave them. You got to have a little sense.

So they argued and finally my grandfather said, Everything you say may be true. And my sheep may die. But I'll tell you one thing. When my last sheep dies, I will be here to skin it.

That's just about the way it ended up. But in the spring he still had the pelts. The wolves didn't get them. So he used that for a new start.

Well, maybe that wasn't a perverse thing. But it was a gritty thing to do. Because his life was really on the line. His life!

So many people I know who are the third-generation ranchers don't really know where that place of theirs came from. They think the damn place fell out of the sky. And the Lord said, I Bestow This on You! They don't know that some old guy, with a gimpy leg, rode around on a horse when it was twenty-two below zero, for all of his lifetime, just to build that ranch. They don't know the amount of deprivation and innovation and dedication that it took for the two generations prior to mine to keep that outfit together.

Nobody my age remembers. People's memories are pretty short.

And maybe we ranchers are so taciturn that we don't pass our tradition, our rural tradition, on to our kids. Maybe I'm lucky, because my folks did talk a lot about the old days, the hard times, the bad times. They taught me that it wasn't all going to be sweetness and light. But a lot of folks here have lost that knowledge of rural traditions.

Folks say to me they don't understand how I can take so much time away from my ranch to fight these coal companies and their strip mines. And what they don't understand is that fighting strip mines, in 1986, is as much an aspect of ranching, as fighting blizzards was in 1886. That is a force a rancher just has to grapple with and resist. Like grasshoppers. Like a drought. Like tough winters.

It's an aspect of ranching. It's not peripheral to ranching. It's an integral part of my being able to stay here and my keeping up my grandfather's tradition and doing what it is I do.

Now, I suppose it's a genetic conspiracy. Maybe I'm just perverse, the way my grandfather was.

"Nothing in the Bible, not even the flight from Egypt, compares to the western movement in the United States in the late 1870s and early 1880s. There never was a movement so vast and so meaningful as the wagon trains coming west. . . ." The rhetorical words of a nineteenth-century prophet of Manifest Destiny? Not at all. They are the down-to-earth judgments of Harry Chrisman, a rancher's son, born in a sod hut near Broken Bow, Nebraska, a man not given to romanticism.

Despite their biblical feat, these homesteaders were hardly biblical heroes to Chrisman. He knew them too well. From the vantage point of his modern log cabin in the hills above Denver, Colorado, he looked back on the pioneering days of his family with critical, but sympathetic, eyes.

And he wondered aloud how people so ordinary could have done the extraordinary things they did. He was not sure he knew the answer. The homesteaders that he had known, what kind of people were they, and why did they do the things they did, and how were they able to endure the suffering they had to, to survive?

Recently, in The New York Times, *John Chamberlain called the old days of ranching "our Homeric age." But Harry Chrisman wasn't sure. What would he call the homesteaders?*

"Peasants," he said.

The Peasants
Harry Chrisman

My family were cattle people, from out in the hills, north of Broken Bow, Nebraska. They lived in soddies. In sod huts. I was born in a soddy. And they didn't go to church. And some of the men didn't even believe in their children going to the school.

They were peasants, in a way.

And why did they come there? They came because they were starved out, and they were kicked out, of wherever they had been resting.

They didn't just come out for the land. They came because other people came. They came for adventure. People came for all sorts of reasons. People from all over the world. People setting up new homes. There's probably hundreds of reasons that people came.

And people who have the stories of their ancestors who came in covered wagons then they ought to tell something about it. To tell how it really was.

And I remember my father saying how the first blizzards he had in Nebraska had decimated his herd. He had brought eight, or nine, hundred head of purebred Durham cattle from Texas. And he lost about one-third of them in the first winter of 1882, I believe it was, in blizzards.

There was a saying that the Chrismans laid up enough sod in that spring of 1883 to fence Custer County. They put up all kinds of barns and sheds and protecting fences. Made of sod. That's all they had to work with. They didn't have any lumber or anything. So they saved their cattle until the next year.

But it was just make-do. My father would always say, Well, if we can just get by till spring!

Come on! he'd say; if we can just get by this winter, why, maybe something will happen.

And it was the same way with the weather. Mark Twain, he said, they always talked about it, but they didn't do anything about it; well, the weather was about all they had to talk about. And they couldn't control the weather and they didn't try to control their farming operations, hardly.

They worked just like their ancestors did. They made-do.

And to make-do was to get by; to use anything that comes to hand. And you saved everything. Even saved a piece of string. And you'd start with the head of a match and wind the string round it and pretty soon you'd have a ball of string, a foot in diameter. And men did the same with a piece of wire or leather. Everything would always serve some purpose or other.

And that was the make-do of those pioneers.

My father's people were Virginian, but he was born in Missouri. And he was just like the old Missouri "stick-in-the-mud" people.

And he won't change. He wouldn't even drive a car. He wouldn't have anything to do with motorized machinery. He was the first man in his neighborhood to have a mechanized haybinder. But he knew so much about horses and so little about machinery that he was perplexed by that machine.

Many of those people seemed to me to be that same way. They wanted to get into that rut, and stay in it, until they couldn't see over the edge of it. And to never do anything different. Just to preserve. To get by. To make-do.

There was a lot of puritanism in many of the pioneer people. There still is.

And I can remember how those people were. They were so wrapped up in their own little world and their own doings, I can't help but say that I almost do feel sorry for them. Because there is a big world around us. And there were, and are, so many things going on politically and economically that could help them. But they want to stick by the kerosene lantern. They just want to go out in the cold and suffer.

These ranch people, they are amazing people to me. They are actually of a real peasant type. They have what you could almost call a peasant attitude.

And that is something to think about, that our own ancestors, our own people, our own fathers and mothers, they were that way.

They still are, in their hearts.

On the famous old wagon trails to the West, the pioneers and settlers mostly followed the trails made by the Indians. They guided them to the best water holes and springs. They led them to the easiest river crossings. They showed them the way over the passes and through the highest mountains. And they led them to the most fertile valleys.

It was almost as if the Indians had unknowingly taken the pioneers by the hand.

Many of the old homesteaders don't see it that way. They might be uncomfortable with the memory, if they did.

One who speaks well and generously of what he learned from the Indians is old Frank Shiveley. In the Nevada territories, where as a young man he and his wife homesteaded, he learned from the ways of the Indians. Since he is proudest of the hand-made leather lariats he braids, to this day, the master craftsman of the lost art, it was his memory of what he learned about the tanning of leather that he recalled and told about most vividly.

But Shiveley is straightforward about everything. So, why not the Indians.

On Learning from the Indians
Frank Shiveley

Once, when I was a kid, I was riding up on the reserve, at one time. There was this old tenter, that was an old Indian, by the creek there. There was this old squaw sitting on the ground. I tried to talk to them, but they wouldn't talk much. Then, I noticed a number of deerskin hides in the creek. They had rocks on them to hold them. Now, one hundred years later I was tanning some deer hides and I thought about doing that. Those Indians had those deer hides in the creek, to soak the hairs off.

And that's how I learned to do tanning in that way.

Sometime later, I seen where this old friend of mine, he was teaching tanning and rawhide at the college up in Elko. And he was using deer hide.

And I says to him, Joe, I can take the hair off it, easier.

And he says, With ashes?

And I says, No, I can take it off easier than that. With running water in the river. Just tie the hides down there and let the water run over it and the hair will come off.

And he says, Yes, I know it.

But he didn't do it. I don't know why. Maybe because that's the Indian ways. But using ashes is a dirty job. And you take the grain off the leather with ash. In the river the leather will score pretty easy and soft.

Those old Indians knew that.

Remember old Garcia, he was an old famous saddle maker? He won first prize at the St. Louis Fair, that was in 1904, with his old $5,000 saddle. That saddle had silver and gold and even diamonds in the conchos. I heard awhile back that saddle was worth $50,000 now. Well, one time he said that his downfall was when he was tanning his own leather. And was using sagebrush ashes. It made for pretty poor leather.

But I liked the Indian way.

Sometimes I would take hides down to this drain here, full of irrigation water. I would take a dry hide and tie it up where it was under water. That water it was pretty fast there. And in six days or so the hair would come off that hide as slick as glass.

One time, I first put a fawn hide in the creek. And I went to town for about a week. When I came back and looked down at that hide, there was nothing but a little old white streak and it was kind of frazzled out. I wondered if some darn fish had been kind of nibbling on it.

But I learned how to do it.

Then, one time, I had four deer hides hanging in the water down there. And when I went down there to get them, they was all gone. Some guy went to stealing them.

So I had to quit doing that.

In the old days there wasn't so much stealing because there wasn't so much people living around. That's why those Indians could do it that way.

"Form a circle or square with your wagons at night," advised one pioneer on the Oregon Trail in 1846, not to guard against Indian attack but "to keep your stock out of camp." If you do not, J. M. Shiveley warned, "you will find your cattle, horses and mules will often take fright at night and run into camp with great fury." Even if "there are no Indians."

It is a wonderful image. The stalwart pioneers forming a circle at night, with their wagons, and standing guard against their own cows.

But in talking to dozens of homesteading families I did not meet a single rancher who told of his ancestors having "trouble" with Indians. Some may have, but no one thought it worth mentioning. There were several old-timers who did remember that the Indians were among the first vaqueros, cowboys on their grandfathers' ranches. Just ranch hands.

There was an old pioneer song that Montana rancher, Spike Van Cleve, recalled:

> *Oh, the Indians 'n the cowboys*
> *They used to live in peace*
> *Till the goddamned dryland farmers*
> *Come adriftin' from the East.*

And Robert Skinner, Sr., remembered that when his grandfather came down the Oregon Trail and homesteaded in eastern Oregon it was the Indians from a nearby tribe who were hired to clear the land, locate the water holes, and help the white man survive.

"Them Indians sure helped us," he said.

The Indians Cleared This Land
   Robert Skinner, Sr.

None of this land was plowed until my grandfather came here. The Indians they made it possible.

The Indians cleared this land. My grandfather hired a bunch of these Paiutes to clear off the sagebrush and they did. Some of them dug a kinda foundation, a cellar, a few feet deep, and they stretched the canvas of two tents over it. And they set up wigwams, all around.

One of their little boys got sick and he died. So they burned down their tents and their wigwams. Burned them all down. It was the only way that they had of getting rid of the germs was the way I figured it. But maybe they were burning out the Death Spirits.

But they worked hard. They was hard workers.

Anyway, it was those Indians who cleared off the sage for us. There never was any trouble with Indians around here, like in the movies.

The Old Days

3

On the Ranch We Were Pretty Damn Self-Sufficient
William Lumpkin

My father's ranch was one hundred miles from town. It took all day to get there. That was Holbrook, Arizona, which I thought was the largest city in the United States, until I was ten. Oh, there was Springerville, but that was just a small village at the time, where the Udall boys, Stu and Mo, grew up. Julius Becher had a store there that sold salt pork and graham crackers and things like that.

Being isolated, we were pretty damn near self-sufficient. We had to be.

We had big gardens there where we grew all sorts things. And we would store them in our big dugout cellars.

We had a gristmill, a flour mill. I remember when they rationed flour during World War I we weren't affected by it at all. Because we grew our own grain and we ground our own flour.

We had a big icehouse. The walls were insulated with sawdust. It was a double-framed building of wood with twelve inches of sawdust between the wooden walls. And the ice lasted there all summer long.

We made our own soap, you know. It was strong. Every bit of fat would be saved. And we would use those big ash barrels. Burning oak in the smokehouse we'd get this ash when we smoked the meats. Then we would run lye water through the ash. And we would make those big bars of soap, that brown soap that would take the dirt and your hide off at the same time.

The ranch was pretty largely self-sufficient. Even had a little commissary, a store for the ranch hands. Where they could buy most things.

Oh, we had to go to town for tobacco, you know. And sugar.

So the ranch, we sent a freight wagon to town every two weeks during the summer, because with the haying and all we'd have a hundred hands working. So we needed supplies and things.

The wagoneer was old Jeff Hill, who was half-Apache and half-Irish. He had the biggest mustache I have ever seen; it must have measured eighteen inches from tip to tip. And Jeff, he was quite big. He inherited more Irish than Apache, I think.

He was a very interesting man, Jeff was. . . .

I remember he used to make what he called "Apache fiddles." He made them of a reed of some kind. The fiddles would be about three or four inches in diameter. And about six feet long. With a single string on them. And he would always insist on making his one string of cat's gut.

And then he would play the thing. Singing these songs from Ireland. I am sure that must have been Gaelic. Because I know they weren't in English. So he'd sing all these Gaelic songs with that Apache voice he had.

He was quite a wagoneer! And his wagons!

They would string two wagons together and use eight mules to pull them. And the wagoneer rode saddle on the side of the lead horses, you know.

Coming down to the ranch house was a road lined with poplar trees, downhill for about a mile. All of us kids, when we knew Jeff was coming back from town, we'd be out there waiting. When he got to the top of the hill he would stand up high in the saddle, and be cracking his whip, and yelling at the top of his voice, and then he would bring the wagons down the road, in between the poplar trees, just galloping and galloping.

And then he would circle round and round in front of the ranch house and the bunkhouse and the barns, with all us kids running after the wagons. Just yelling our heads off.

Sometimes he would bring us kids an orange. And we would keep that orange for months, before we ate it.

No one looks more like what a rancher is supposed to than William Lumpkin. His white, full mustache. His elegant and low-profiled cowboy hat. His casual western jacket set off by a silk cravat. The Santa Claus wrinkles around his eyes when he smiles. His friendly manner. His love of good talk. The easy way he walks. The modest and quiet manner, so genuine it is deceptive, with which he tells stories of the old days.

But he is no rancher.

And if he portrays his days on the ranch with the artistry of an artist, and sets up the scene like an architect, that's because he is both. He left his father's ranch "too long ago to remember," he says, when they "went broke."

Down in Lincoln County, New Mexico, the Lumpkins were a prominent ranching family before they were wiped out. Bill's uncle had been foreman on the old Matador outfit, while another relative had been a judge in the Billy the Kid days. And his father not only had his own ranch in Lincoln County, but that 250,000-acre spread in the Apache country of Arizona.

Those "great days of ranching" that Lumpkin fondly remembers differ in size and scope from those of smaller ranchers. But that's where the difference ends.

On their little ranch in northern Nevada, where they had one or two ranch hands, not one hundred, Frank and Marian Shiveley made-do in ways very similar to those of the Lumpkins. They had to. They lived eighty miles from the railroad, beyond the stagecoach roads. They sometimes couldn't make it into town at all during the winter.

And so Frank and Marian remembered in greater detail the ways of making-do that Lumpkin knew as a young boy.

Making-Do
Marian and Frank Shiveley
On Making Jelly Jars from Whiskey Bottles

MARIAN: Back in the time when people lived in the country, in our grandmothers' time, you couldn't buy a lot of things. And you couldn't get a lot of jelly jars.

FRANK: There was always lots of old beer bottles around.

MARIAN: You're getting ahead of my story.

FRANK: In those days that was mining country and they had to have saloons and they had lots of bottles.

MARIAN: Anyway, his mother, she would heat the branding iron. She would heat it red-hot. She would have her bottles, beer bottles and whiskey bottles, ready. She had different sizes.

FRANK: She would stick that branding iron in the stove. She would have a good fire. And she would have her bottles lined up on a bench and she would bring that branding iron out and she would just get it down over an old bottle and would hit 'em with an old Case knife.

MARIAN: And the tops of the bottles came off clean. There was no splinters or anything. So they made good jelly and jam jars.

But they didn't have any lids. So they always saved overalls, and if they didn't save the whole overall they would save the legs, and cut out nice squares of that cloth and put them over the tops of those bottles when they were filled and then tie a string around them. Then we bought resin by the cake and melted that up and we poured it over the top of that, edges and all.

Now, I never lived where we'd never had jelly jars, but we didn't have lids. So I would save the nice parts of overalls. And it kept just as well as with lids.

FRANK: I don't remember any string on my mother's bottles.

MARIAN: Well, you see, her bottles were different. Ours had a little groove around them. But whiskey bottles don't.

On Refrigeration Without Refrigerators

MARIAN: Now, about keeping meat. If we quartered a cow we always had some muslin to wrap it in to keep the flies away. Then we would hang the quarters out in the night. In the morning we would sack it and put it in the cellar. And if we didn't have a cellar, like in buckaroo camps and in hay camps, why, they'd sack the meat and put it in the shade, under hay, and keep it in there all day.

And, in the night, they'd hang it up in the trees.

That's how we kept meat before we had refrigeration. Which was a long time.

FRANK: And most ranches had canvas meat sacks and you'd put a quarter of the cow in that and tie it so no bugs or flies could get to it, and roll it up in the canvas.

MARIAN: And how did you do it when you were out in camp?

FRANK: On buckaroo wagons, we would hang the meat up at night, right on the wagons. So it would cool off. We would kill the meat at night. And in the mornings we would put it underneath the wagons, in the shade, and the cook would have to keep it there when the sun was shining.

And, oh, ya, we used to salt the meat in whiskey barrels. When you cut a piece of meat you'd take it out of the barrels and have to soak it in fresh water, or maybe boil the salt off it.

But it was still pretty salty. No matter what.

MARIAN: One time, as I remember, we fixed up a screen cupboard. We had shelves in it. And we could put our milk there and anything else we wanted to keep cool. Then we put a blanket over it, or several thicknesses of burlap, from new sacks.

On the top of the screen cupboard we had a five-gallon can of water with little holes in it, little bitty leaks to keep it dripping and keep it wet all day. The nice thing about it was that it was in the shade, right close to the spring, so right about the time you figured the well was going dry you'd get some water in that can.

And that was nice.

FRANK: One fellow told me once about making beef jerky. The way you do it is to kill the animal and cut the meat in strips and hang it out to dry and put it away the same day. You always had to cut the meat sideways.

MARIAN: Why?

FRANK: I don't know why, ma'am. That is just the way they did it.

On Cooking on a Fireless Stove

MARIAN: Now I will go to the fireless cooker. Have you ever had a fireless cooker?

Well, when I was growing up we had the fireless cooker to save the wood and the heat in the summer. We always seemed to have plenty of wood. But in the summer, we just didn't burn it because we were conservative.

And so we took some nice and flat rocks, and in the morning when we used the oven for breakfast we put a flat rock in there, or if there was no room in the oven we put a flat rock on top. When the rock was good and hot we took that rock outside, right close to the house, and we put the meat and beans for lunch on that rock and covered it with a blanket. And we would leave it until noon, and your meat was done and your beans were done. And if you took garden things, or opened a can or something, it wouldn't take them long to get done.

And we had one fireless cooker, it was made of metal and it had three compartments, a big one in the middle and two small ones on either side. If we wanted to put three things in there, we could.

So that's what we did.

FRANK: Once I worked for an old uncle. And his wife had a fireless cooker. It was a square box, coated with aluminum or something, and the top fastened down with clamps and it had a pop-off button like these pressure cookers.

And one time I made my own. I was out in a buffalo camp.

I had a buffalo camp where I been dug in there against a bank. And I made this fireless cooker of a piece of tin. Well, I put that up against the bank and cooked on that. Well, I would get a pot of beans started to boil in the morning and set them in there and clamp the lid down and go off riding and when you come in about four o'clock in the afternoon, why all your beans'd be ready.

Some boy, he brought a little cookbook over to camp, one time. And we looked through the cookbook and said, We'll make a cake. So we put that cake in that fireless cooker. And we were going out to make a ride, figuring to be back around two that afternoon.

Well, where the camp was, the creek dropped off pretty fast, down And when we were coming back I smelled something awful good. We had put a little vanilla in that cake and that was what was poppin' off in there. It was just like a scent to bring a coyote to the trap. And when we opened the lid that cake browned and cooked just as nice as you could cook.

MARIAN: That was a big thing, in those days, to have that. You know, I'm kind of sorry that we don't have a fireless cooker anymore. Though we don't need it, it would be fun to have.

On Freeze-Drying in the Snow

MARIAN: My mother used to put the dish towels, if they didn't look real good, out on the snow to freeze-dry. And lots of times right today I will let my sheets out on the line, to freeze-dry. It bleaches them. And it isn't near as hard on them as Clorox and those bleaches.

On Making Soap

MARIAN: Now, we were thinking back to Frank's grandmother making lye to make soap. She would say, I am out of lye and I got to make some lye. She had this five-gallon can with a bunch of holes poked in it. And she would take these wood ashes, and put them in there and pour some water through those wood ashes and that water soaking through those wood ashes leaked out through the holes and it took the lye out with it.

She had to pour the water through there several times, so that she would have the strength in the lye.

FRANK: Those were just common wood ashes. Any wood ashes that would be handy to use.

MARIAN: And that lye soap was good as a bleach. In those days we didn't have any Clorox and all that. So that soap was soap and bleach in one. And it was so easy to make. All you needed was a little water and some wood ashes and a little bit of animal fat.

And you had soap.

On Making Whiskey

FRANK: In our country there was no law about making whiskey. So we had some of the best moonshine there was. Everybody was entitled to make all that he wanted to drink. One of the boys that I knew, he said, I'm a producer and I'm a consumer, but I can consume more than I can produce.

Now, how do you make whiskey? It's easy enough. All you do is you take some wheat, cracked wheat that's ground up. And sugar.

More sugar than anything. And then you cook it up until it's hot enough to ferment. It'll take a few days afore it ferments. And after it ferments you dip your hand in it and if it dries off pretty quick, it's ready. So you put it in your still. You got to have a coil. The still is a pot with a dome on it and a coil for the cool water, so that the steam of the fermented sugar and wheat comes out like liquid. And that's whiskey.

In the old days we had a still in the tie house, down in the flats. Nobody come there in winter. And if they did, we just throwed a horse blanket over it. It smelled corny when we cooked the whiskey but we always cooked it at night.

One feller down below Bunkerville [Nevada], one time, he was making whiskey. He'd get this cracked corn. And he'd be drinking that still until his teeth turned black. He'd say, I feel like I'm salivated. And I'd say, You sort of look it too.

And, one time, after we had an awful hard winter, in 1916 or 1917, all the Charleston people were out haying and they took some whiskey downriver, down the Diamond desert and down the breaks and all the way down there. And I was down there in that spring gatherin' cattle. I was the "Rep" down there. And we'd see the mule trains going across to Idaho on those old roads. And they'd load whiskey on the mules and take it to Idaho.

Everybody was drunk all the time, down there. Never had to buy anything. The young fellers'd give you a quart, figure you'd keep your mouth shut.

One of the funniest things was, I remember, when the country was going dry, one of the biggest stills in the county was in the basement of the county courthouse. It was the safest place. No one'd get arrested there.

On ranches from Montana to Texas many of the problems the ranchers faced were similar, but not the same. Even so, on their own and unknown to each other, they often came to similar conclusions and solutions. And though men or women would make-do in their own way, whatever way they could, there seemed to be general rules their individuality obeyed.

"There are just so many ways that you can kill a coyote dead,"one rancher said.

But the physical ways of making-do by doing this or that were no more, and maybe less unique than the way the doer looked at it. Making-do was a way of thinking that was inherently conservationist. It was not the idea of making something out of nothing. Rather, it was, as Tug Pettit remembered it, making "something out of something." Of conserving what you had. That is, it was utilitarian, functional, puritanical, practical, and useful.

In west Texas, that flat, dry, hard, stubborn land where Ruth and Tug Pettit grew up, these characteristics of making-do were unforgiving.

Something Out of Something
Tug and Ruth Pettit
On Making Machines

TUG: We had to figure out some way of making something out of something. Or other.

I never will forget when we put in some farmland, we'd make three rounds in the field with the turning plow. To turn over the sod. And then we'd take an old, tin dishpan and put a plate over it, and drill holes in it, and put corks in the holes and fill that up with seeds, and hitch it up to the plow, and follow the rows around like that. It was a good planter. It made a good seeder.

Yah, just an old dishpan.

And I remember when we got to farming quite a bit and we eventually got a good little blacksmith shop on the ranch. Well, there was no place to go to get your tool sharp. Dad, he knew how to make horseshoes and he had shoed horses.

One time I needed something welded together. And we didn't have nothing to weld with but this white sand, just clean, good white sand. Now, a lot of people they would think you're crazy if you tried to weld with sand. But, Dad, he'd say, All right, I'll just show you! And he'd have a good furnace and get it red-hot and put a little sand on it and when it got ready he'd jerk it out on the anvil and beat it down. And he had a weld.

Later, when cars come in, he repaired car parts in that blacksmith shop. Instead of horses.

The first car my dad bought was a two-cylinder Buick. Cranked on the side. Run by chain. And from that he went to an old Hudson. And that old Hudson, it done all right until the flu epidemic of '18 when we used to haul coffins in it. The flu hit our country and we had the fever and, oh, my God! we'd haul two coffins at a time, crosswise in that car.

But, that darn thing would freeze up on us. Right while we were ahauling those coffins.

So I said, Let's drain the water out of that car and fill it up with coal oil. That coal oil wouldn't freeze. And so we did that.

And we just wrapped ropes around the wheels to make mud chains. And we'd go off.

And just like we used to grease a wagon wheel with bacon, we'd use the bacon on the tires. To shrink them and to make them fit. Later we used bacon on the old Model-T bands; the bacon rind, it worked good on that.

RUTH: Making-do in west Texas, well, there wasn't much to make-do with.

On Curing Meat

TUG: Oh, yah, it was real dry there where we were. In west Texas.

Beef, we just drawed it up and hung it up on the windmill tower with a slicker around it. That's all. Either a slicker or canvas or sheet or whatever you had. It'd dry on the outside. And we drawed it up under the platform of the windmill, so it didn't get wet anyway. And it just seemed to cure itself.

RUTH: The beef just hung out there on the windmill.

TUG: And it'd cure itself in the sun and wind. Nothing could get at it, up there on the windmill.

RUTH: And we cured our own pork. I remember Grandpa always put out the long boards. And we'd have a big hog killing. And we'd mix up salt and cayenne pepper and sugar and we'd rub it and rub it and rub it on the hogs and then turn them over and rub it on their backs. And then we'd hang them up in the smokehouse. We called it that, even though it wasn't.

TUG: Sometimes we packed the pork down in a barrel of salt. And made salt pork. In a big barrel you could put three hams in there and cover them up with the salt.

RUTH: And my mother, she would fry sausage we made. She would put the fried sausage in big crock jars and pour lard in on top and cover them up.

And the meat would keep that way even in summer.

On Keeping Milk Fresh

RUTH: Milk, the way they'd keep it fresh was in the windmills. They'd build a big old trough, about so wide and so deep. And the water pumped up by the windmill, it would run through there. And they would set the milk vessels in there. And cover the trough with a cloth. And it would be colder than a refrigerator.

TUG: Of course you had to keep the kids from going out there and skimming the cream off.

RUTH: And you know how they'd do that?

TUG: The kids'd take a long macaroni. Like a straw. And they'd stick it in the milk there and skim off the cream. Suck off all the cream.

RUTH: And if the milk got sour we made cupboard cheese, what is called cottage cheese. You took some sour milk at a certain temperature and you put it in a flour sack and hung it on the clothesline. In a day or so you'd have a real good cheese.

And the kids, they didn't try to steal that.

On a ranch the first car, often as not, was parked in the barn with the buggies and wagons. The horses would have to move over.

And if the ranchers at times seemed to treat those early cars like a horse and wagon and drive them like buggies, it may have been because, as William Lumpkin remembers them, they "looked a lot like old buggies." So the ranchers did everything but feed them oats.

In those days cars had not become the status or sex symbols they are now. They were simply mechanical workhorses. And they were made so almost anyone could repair them, if they broke down.

"That was an advantage," said Bill Lumpkin. "If your car broke down on the road you didn't have to shoot it."

Buggies and Cars
William Lumpkin

One day when we were driving back to the ranch from town in the old Model-T, we ran out of oil. We had apparently run over a rock and knocked the lower cog off the oil pan and drained out all the oil. And we had burned out the bearings, too. Well, in those days you always carried some bacon, a little something to eat, you know. So we skinned the skin off the bacon and put it in the sockets where the bearings were and tied it on.

And we drove on into the ranch.

That day, my father and brothers and I, we had gone down

to Holbrook. And we were coming back when the oil gave out. The old Model-T had a little cog down the side of the oil pan, it had two of them. If you turned the top one and no oil drained out, then you turned the bottom one, and if no oil drained out you was out of oil. And you filled it to the top, until it started to run over. That was how you measured the oil.

On the Model-T and the Model-A, you know, you could literally repair them on the road. They were built that way, so anyone could repair them, even if you were in the middle of nowhere, which was where you most often was.

And you never had to carry a jack. You just carried a big block. Because a man, one man, could lift those cars up, so you lifted it up and put the block under and changed a wheel, and kicked the block out, and went on.

In those days cars looked a lot like buggies. The first car I ever saw had no doors; it was a two-seater, and it had a front and back seat set in the open air, like a buggy, and it had a stiff, high top with tassels around it. And it had big old back wheels and little bitty front wheels, with hard tires, just like a buggy.

And it had carbide lights on it that you lit with a match. Like a kerosene lamp.

The only thing that that car didn't have was a horse.

The good old-fashioned home medicines that most people like to remember were composed of aromatic herbs and wise folk sayings. But most folk remedies were not like that at all.

One remedy for a cut, or wound, was to fill it "with spit or manure," or "let a dog lick it clean." An old-time cure for diphtheria was for "the sick person to urinate in a cup of green carrots and hang the cup on the chimney for eight days"; while a popular cure for acne was to "wash your face in a baby diaper wet with urine but not feces."

Some remedies were even more esoteric and mysterious. Like a cure for rheumatism in which the sufferer was told to "put a young Negro boy across the foot of the bed and put your feet

on his back or stomach and the rheumatism will drain into his
body."
    And some folk medicines were quite simple, as Bill Lumpkin
remembers. They simply cleaned out your body of its evil spirits,
and everything else.

It Cured Everything You Had
    William Lumpkin

    In the little Spanish village that was down by the river,
in Martineztown, the flu epidemic of 1918 was just awful. The
people were just dying. People were dying like flies. They were
building coffins out of one-by-four boards, on the assembly line.
Ten or fifteen people were dying there every day.
    We were all going around, you know, with "assfidity" around
our necks. And a mask on our faces.
    My father got hold of Washington, the Public Health Serv-
ice, or something. In those days Washington was everything.
And he got them to ship a doctor out. And he died two days
after he got there. And so they shipped a nurse down.
    Some people said this flu was nothing but the croup. And
castor oil would cure it. And so we sent our ranch foreman, Jeff
Hill, to get four or five cases of castor oil. It took a whole day's
trip, across the Petrified Forest, to get that castor oil.
    When he got back, Jeff threw some of that castor oil in his
saddlebags, and started making the rounds. He gave everybody who had the flu that castor oil. The standard dose of
castor oil was one bottle for one person. And they took it in one
big swallow.
    Now, Jeff bragged he never lost no one. Maybe he was just
lucky. I don't know.
    And then there was Syrup of Figs. Syrup of Figs! I guess it
was an extract of figs. You took a double spoonful and just
camped out by the outhouse. And it cured everything you might
have, just the way castor oil did.
    They told about a cowboy that took a big dose of Syrup of
Figs. Well, our old bunkhouse was on one side of a big irriga-

tion ditch, a hundred yards to cross over to the outhouse. It drained off down the hog pen. At about midnight, this cowboy, who took the Syrup of Figs, was tearing on down the irrigation ditch, and as he come around the ditch he slipped, and fell. He got up and said, Well, I wouldn't have made it anyway.

And he sauntered off.

On many old ranches the wood cookstoves sit in the kitchen beside the new electric and gas ranges. They often haven't been used in years. Sometimes they've been exiled to barns and sheds, with dusty saddles and broken buggies. One family I know keeps its cookstove not for cooking, but for heating up their morning coffee, by burning their daily junk mail.

Not so the Spragues. On their family ranch, the wood cookstove is the heart of their homestead.

To Virginia and Harold Sprague, burning wood in their cookstove isn't a matter of nostalgia. Nor ecology. Nor just economy. Nor do they do it simply to take the chill out of the Montana mornings. Though that helps.

As far as they can see they use the wood cookstove for "human reasons." For the same reason they have no electricity; it expresses what they think about ranching, and their way of living, better than any words could do.

We Have No Electricity
Virginia and Harold Sprague

VIRGINIA: Our way of living? We like to live this way, out in the country, away from people. We have no electricity. We have no electricity bills, either. We have no TV. We have peace of mind. We are our own boss. Other than that we have our horses and cattle. We have this cozy old ranch house; it's really a log cabin from homesteading days. And we just like it out here, I guess.

HAROLD: Sure thing.

VIRGINIA: If we wanted to stay in bed until ten in the morning, we can. And we don't have to go out and punch a time clock. I've done that, too. I lived right in downtown St. Louis for three or four years. And I worked there and had electricity and all the conveniences; but I do not mind being without them, here. It might be nice to have electricity, but we can't afford it on this size place we got.

Besides, I like using this old wood cookstove, here.

HAROLD: And I can work all I want to. When I want to. If I feel like it, I can work hard and put in a long day, and if I don't feel like it, I can just put in a short day. I got a heart condition, and that's one of the things that makes it good to work that way.

VIRGINIA: We can live here, and we can make a living, and not *just* work. Though we can't live like a lot of people would like to.

Someone, I suppose he was an official at the Colstrip power plant, where our son works, he said, Why, people can't live without electricity! And so our son said, Oh, yes, they can! I know of some people that live without electricity! And this official, he wanted to know where they lived. And Roger, our son, said, They live seventeen miles from this power plant! And so, this official asked him, Do they live like people? So our son said, Oh, sure, they're my mother and father!

And that official, he just couldn't believe it.

But we like to live this way we do, for human reasons. In some ways, it's more human to not have electricity.

Now, you take what is it we like about this cookstove. With a wood, or coal, fire you can back up to it and warm the seat of your pants. Harold says he likes to back up to it and get the rivets in his Levi's warm.

And you can't do it the same way with a gas or electric heater. It don't feel at all the same.

HAROLD: See, the cookstove, that's a personal thing. It's got a different feeling from electricity.

VIRGINIA: So, in the wintertimes, we use this wood cookstove here in the kitchen for heat. And cooking. And then we have a coal stove in the living room to heat that with.

HAROLD: And we got wood all over this outfit. Some of it is more or less in our way. It lays up in the old creeks and you get a fast rain and then it comes down and washes out the fences. It ought to be used.

VIRGINIA: A young man who works for Wally, he's our neighbor, he lives in a modern house, but they have an old cookstove in the kitchen. For extra heat in wintertime. And it's nice to keep a kettle on.

HAROLD: Well, you know, I think that may be a good thing. The way a lot of the young people are trying the old things. It may help on this here so-called energy, so-called crisis.

VIRGINIA: Besides, our grandchildren like to play in the wood-box when it is empty. They play jack-in-the-box. Come popping out of there and scare you near to death.

HAROLD: A wood cookstove, it's just more of a family thing. Friendlier than a lot of electricity. Most people won't know what we are talking about. That is right. There is no way for them to know what we've just said. It's just words to them. And it doesn't tell them anything.

The old days are long gone, forgotten, vanished, lost. And yet, they sometimes reappear in the most unlikely places.

Sitting in the air-conditioned living room of a modern ranch house, in between a large-screen television set and an ornamental fireplace, while waiting for the women in their Good Housekeeping *kitchens to prepare lunch, may seem a paradoxical setting to sit around in and discuss the wonders of the old days, when men and women on a ranch had to make-do.*

But, when the Skinner family gathers for lunch, the old days and the new days inevitably get together as well. For there are three generations of Skinners sitting at the table of their new ranch house, just across from where the old ranch house once stood; grandfather, father, and son.

And so the conversation is unique in the way it goes from memories of the old days to the realities of today.

And We Could Do It Again
Robert Skinner, Sr., Robert Skinner, Jr., and Son

GRANDFATHER: One time my father had a crew of forty people working on this ranch. Feeding that bunch of people was quite a problem, you know. Once a year we hitched up the six-horse team and went into town, and we would stock up. And it was lot different than it is now when you can go to the store every few days, just drive to town and get what you want.

So we made-do on the ranch. Best we could. We had to.

FATHER: As a boy, I do remember the teams bringing the supplies in. And backing up to the basement door of the ranch house. And carrying the sacks of flour 'n things down the basement. And those big cans of beans and macaroni. When the supplies came in you always had things to eat you didn't have all year.

That was for sure!

GRANDFATHER: With a crew like that you didn't need a lot of refrigeration. The meat, it would only last a week. And we had an agreement with the neighboring ranch, where they and we would alternate killing a beef a week and sharing it, half and half. And a week, that was as long as a beef would need to last.

On cool nights we would hang a beef out, to keep it. And in the daytime we would wrap it up and put it in the shade. But as I said, it didn't last long.

Then we would cure a hundred hogs a year. And make our own bacon and hams and sausage.

FATHER: They had an icebox in the big ranch house. And as long as they had ice it worked pretty good. It had two compartments that were built into the house. Like rooms.

Sometimes we cut ice for it at Cow Creek. It kept things pretty cool.

GRANDFATHER: In the wintertimes, we would put up that ice. And we would use a room in the granary as an icehouse. Packed the ice in straw. But, in the summertime there was no refrigeration except in the well. We kept the butter there.

FATHER: They had their own dairy on the ranch, then. And they made all of their own butter. And things.

On the ranches they were pretty self-sufficient in those days. They did buy, oh, flour and beans and sugar and rice and coffee and fruits and things like that. But all these ranches were pretty self-sufficient. Most of the time. They learned how to get by with what they had, and make-do.

GRANDFATHER: I think that had a lot to do with the independent spirit of ranchers. Absolutely!

FATHER: If the energy crisis was to get worse and the electricity was to give out, I think we could do that again. Yes, I believe we could pull through. It would be hard. But, I think we'd still have the basic knowledge of how to be self-sufficient. Maybe we'd have to do some changing in the way we live, the way we operate this ranch, but it wouldn't all be for the worst, as I see it.

Maybe the people in the cities, they wouldn't get by. But we would.

SON: If we did that, don't you think the city people might just come out here to take it from us?

GRANDFATHER: That's a thought.

Communities
of Rugged
Individualists

4

On Cattle Drives
Frank and Marian Shiveley
Tug and Ruth Pettit

FRANK: On cattle drives we used to throw our beef in with the rest of them. We'd have a thousand head of beef going up there to the railroads. Steers, cows, bulls and everything, you know. My brothers and my grandfather and my uncles and a neighbor or two, we'd all get together on cattle drive.

MARIAN: For the first few years we kinda all lived together in the family. Our ranches all had kinda run together, you know.

And then we divided the ranches. They had the lower ranch and we had the upper ranch. But we were still family, you know.

FRANK: And what beat us back was these two uncles. On a cattle drive, as far as being leaders for a bunch of cattle, you ought to ride on the side and let everything stay cooped up and not run off with them. But these two uncles they'd just go as fast as they'd go. So, when they'd get to the next camp, they'd have only maybe twenty head. When they'd go riding off, they'd just turn their back on them cattle. They wouldn't pick 'em up. And they'd go on.

On cattle drives you don't go ride off, fast, by yourself. Everybody, they's got to be together.

Well, as you went on there was a little old pass there, in the mountains, and they'd go over that and start buttoning up your coat. They'd go over the summit there, and then it'd be four or six miles downhill.

So they'd trot them cattle down there. That's no way to drive beef. It loses meat. Even kills 'em.

And so we said to heck with them. One year we saw some truckers down there. They'd started to truck beef. And we said next year we'd truck our beef that way. So we built a loading corral.

From then on we trucked our beef by ourself. Neighbors did the same. And there was no more of the old-time cattle drives. Everyone was on his own.

There was a fellow there who had sold his ranch and he was running scales in Elko and he saw a lot of cattle come in there. He told us, You boys had the best cattle come in these yards.

I says, Better than the YP ranch?

He says, Oh, hell! The YP don't have cattle near like yours.

The day we was there folks'd keep saying, Whose cattle is them?

We says, Them's mine.

They says, Where'd you get 'em?

We says, Oh, they come from our upper ranch. You ought to see them we got down on the lower place.

The great herds of cattle thundered across the plains. On the cattle drives there seemed to be thousands of head that stretched as far as the horizon and the dust they raised was like a storm cloud. All around them rode the cowboys like a phalanx of soldiers who protected the cattle from the elements and Indians and themselves.

It is one of the dramatic scenes of the Old West, those cattle drives.

But there weren't that many cattle ranches that big. Nor could the ordinary rancher afford to hire a John Wayne as his drive boss.

Most of the old-time ranchers and homesteads were not very big. A family might have a few dozen, or a few hundred, head of cattle. Of those not all would be sent to market, but mostly the calves and steers.

*And so, the way Marian and Frank Shiveley remembered it,
families and their friends had to get together on a cattle drive.
"Everybody, they's got to be together," as Frank said, or they
could not survive.*

*The ranchers had to stick together, they were too poor not
to. For "to be too individualistic" just made things harder,
Frank Shiveley said, and life was "pretty rugged" without any
of that.*

*"Even the most individualistic so-and-so worked together,"
Tug Pettit said. Not because he liked to but because he had to.
He had no choice. If he didn't cooperate with his neighbors he
couldn't have been the rugged individualist that he was.*

*Ruth and Tug Pettit remembered even more of that kind of
sharing. Not only on the cattle drives but when haying or out
branding or on roundups, whole families helped one another.*

RUTH: In those days they used to have big roundups.
Each rancher he would pick a day. And everybody would go
over to his place to help him on his roundup. They'd kill a beef.
Have a barbecue.

TUG: And neighbors they all helped each other getting their
stuff to market. On cattle drives they drove several days, together, on horseback and wagon. We'd take cows and calves
and all. Just graze them along easy. In order to hold flesh on
the calves.

We carried feed and water. And we carried our own shade.
For the heat of the day. On those plains shade was a scarce
commodity. And there weren't any springs or water.

That cattle drive was almost forty miles to the railroad. That
was up in Canyon, Texas, just south of Amarillo, near the old
Goodnight Ranch.

And when we'd get there, we would ship the calves and bring
the cows home. Oh, we would have a hallelujah of a time, then,
because those cows wanted to go back to where we left their
babies, you know. So that wasn't easy.

RUTH: It was slow going. Not like in the movies.

The small ranchers had to be good neighbors. It was most often the surest way to preserve their economic independence. So, in a way, the ability to be rugged individualists was based on a capacity to be a cooperative neighbor. In the ranching communities, the rural towns, the farm organizations, the marketing cooperatives, and the early Populist movements, the independence and dependence of homesteading ranchers was more than a matter of economic necessity. It grew into a way of life.

On the self-sufficient large ranches the need for independence and cooperation was even more obvious. The vast spreads were communities unto themselves. And the cowhands, those most individualistic of men, had to work in coordinated teams. The loner might be the hero of the easterner who dreamed of escaping from the confines of urban life, but on a large ranch at calfing or roundup time the loner "wasn't worth his own dirt," as an old-time rancher recalled.

And when a catastrophe hit a big ranch it was little different than if it struck a small one. Neighbors came from miles around to help out, as William Lumpkin recalls happened on one of his father's holdings in Arizona, back in the days before anyone heard of depending on disaster help from the government.

"Folks had to help out each other," Lumpkin said. "No one else would."

The Night Our Herd Went Through the Ice, Everybody Came to Help
William Lumpkin

One winter we almost lost our entire herd of Hereford cattle. They nearly drowned.

There was a volcanic mesa on the flats, near Springerville. We pulled the water up out of the Little Colorado River, there, and used it to irrigate our alfalfa fields. When we didn't need the water we would run it into these sinkholes and make little lakes. Some were pretty big lakes. And in the winter these lakes would freeze over.

Every morning we would go out and chop holes in the ice. So those cattle could drink.

And then this snowstorm came. It was heavy snow. And it started to drift over the lakes, so the cows didn't recognize there was ice underneath. 'Cause a cow won't go on ice, you know.

Well, a couple hundred head went out on the ice. That morning, whoever it was who went out to cut some ice, all he saw was a couple hundred cows' heads all sticking up out of the ice.

Bellowing! And roaring!

It had snowed all that night. And that lake was about a mile and a half from the ranch house. But everyone went tearing out of the ranch house to help.

Even when we'd got some cows out they were so cold and charred we had to build big bonfires to warm them. In all about two hundred head went in. And we'd lost about a hundred. Two of them were prize bulls.

All that day and the next night we were fishing cows out. If they'd drowned we left them there and came back in a day or two to get their hides.

Some people had gone to town to get help. And neighbors came.

There must have been hundreds, hundreds of people, who came out to the ranch to help that night. Everybody came to help. Women came out. They was cooking and making coffee all night.

One of these blizzard type of snow storms hit that country from time to time, all that time the storm was going on and on. But those people stayed and helped us, even so. It was like that, in those days, you know.

This news story appeared in the Santa Fe New Mexican *on Sunday, March 4, 1979.*

GHOST RANCH, NEW MEXICO: *The old West came alive Saturday at this 21,000-acre ranch north of Abiquiu as more than 30 cowboys rounded up about 400 cows and herded them several miles to a late winter pasture. The cattle belong to 27 northern New Mexico ranchers who keep their livestock on the ranch during the winter. . . .*

It was a contemporary story of an old ranching tradition. The rancher was not only neighborly in a personal way, he shared his ranching problems, and their solutions, with his neighbors as well. If that meant putting in his herd with others for a roundup, or a cattle drive, or protection against a storm, or rustlers, he did that too.

On the frontiers no people developed these communal ways more enthusiastically than did the Mormons. Their communities and their church institutionalized the spirit of cooperation. And they all but moralized the necessity of cooperation into a religious belief, and a moral doctrine.

Stan Jonasson, a young man of old Mormon stock, has restated his ancestors' communal morality in a modern ideological viewpoint that the church may be less than enthusiastic about. But, as he says, "It's interesting."

The Land in Common
Stan Jonasson

Mormons worked the land in common. They had common granaries where it was "each according to his ability, and each according to his need." They had that system for many years. And I don't remember what led to its demise. There was common harvesting. There was the putting-up of whatever was taken from the land—to be shared. And the canning was then done by the women of the Mormon Relief Society, for everyone.

It was. And it still is.

Those people, my ancestors, they were burned out and they had their possessions taken and their lands taken and they had to flee farther and farther west. One group would go ahead and plant the crops and another group would come behind them and harvest the crops and another group would come and winter with the harvest and preserve the food. They would keep on coming, coming in waves, each sharing what another group had worked to produce.

I have an affinity for that whole thing. Yeah, that is a strong part of my background. My grandparents made that a big deal.

Farms were held in common, by the church, in those days. Even now the good LDS, Latter-Day Saints, sometimes have a paid person on their ranch, paid by the church, to oversee their land.

People who are in the church, when they are good LDS, they still work a certain amount of hours for the church. One of the ways to make your "time payment" is to go out and work on a farm. And it is a formalized rural system of sharing the fruit of the earth that is a communal subculture in this part of the country. Especially in eastern Idaho, in Nevada, in Arizona, in Utah.

My family is pretty much from the old ranching and farming communities of that kind. One side of my family is real heavy LDS, in southeastern Idaho, north of Logan, Utah.

They've held high positions in the church. I have a cousin who is next in line to be the president of the LDS, the Mormon Church. His name is Ezra Taft Benson; he used to be Secretary of Agriculture during the presidency of General Eisenhower.

Now, I'm not sure if those Mormon ideas of sharing, whether they are Marxist ideas. But Brigham Young had basically the same ideas.

The phone rang.

It was a neighbor, a rancher down the road, calling to say that he had a grass fire on his place and the fire was threatening one of the wooden bridges he had built over the creek. In two minutes flat, the ranch house had all but emptied out. All of the young men and all of the young children and all of the young women but one had climbed into two pickup trucks and they drove off in a cloud of dust, to fight the fire.

Maybe half an hour or so later they all came back choking somewhat, and spitting out smoke. But they were smiling. They'd put out the fire.

One of the young boys, wiping the soot from his forehead, said, "In a city a man wouldn't hardly know how to put a fire out on his own place. Much less go to help his neighbor. But, out here, on a ranch we don't hardly have no choice. We have to be neighborly.

"Fire engine's in town," he said. "That's thirty miles."

On isolated ranches, far from town, the need for neighborliness lives on. Not just because it's necessary, but because it is a more "satisfying" way of living than being alone, said Ellen Cotton.

"It's a good feeling," she said, "to being neighborly."

On Being Neighborly
Ellen Cotton

One way the rural way of life is satisfying is your neighbors. Because your neighbors depend on you and you depend on them. There is a feeling of need for each other, you have a basic need for each other. And it's a relationship that I think is based on real values, not superficial values.

I live all alone on this place. But I couldn't do it alone. Because a human being wasn't meant to live all by himself.

My neighbors are always calling up and saying, Now, well, don't you go riding off on any horses way up on those pastures without telling us where you are. And they will call up around five o'clock and if I am not home they'll go looking for me. And I am the same way with them.

If they go riding off to some distant cow camp, in iffy weather, they'll call me and say, We're going up to this here place. So, if you call us up around five o'clock and we're not home, we went out in this direction, so you might take a look out that way.

One day last year I went out riding to this pasture and my horse must have bolted me. I don't remember what happened. Because when I was thrown my head must have hit a rock. And I was out cold. The doctor said later I had a brain concussion. Well, my horse went back to the corral alone and they came looking for me.

That may have saved my life.

In this little neighborhood, here, we don't have very many

neighbors. But we are always willing to help each other out.

And we have good times together. But we live very independent lives. And we are always on call. But we don't impinge upon
each other.

And so we help each other and we are fond of each other and
yet we don't impinge on each other's private affairs and stuff
like that. It is very satisfying and nice.

*Once, not too long ago, the quiet valley was crisscrossed
by farms. And up in the foothills, between the waving grasslands and the tall standing forests of evergreens, the ranches
guarded the mountains. The Bitterroot Valley of Montana was
one of those mythic places that people meant when they spoke
of a sense of eternity in the West.*

That eternity has ended. Sooner than we thought it would.

*Now the valley is dotted with colonies of summer homes
and trailer camps. The rustic atmosphere seems to soothe the
urban refugees and many of their vacation homes are built
in the shape of "scientifically engineered" log cabins. On the
old highway there are several manufacturers of prefabricated
log cabins that may be bought in any style or size of "instant
rusticness."*

*But the major change in the valley is not so much the coming
of new ways as the dying of the old ways. The iconoclastic and
independent ranchers and the familylike and neighborly communities they founded seem as out of place as the fake log
cabins.*

*Still, the valley remains the kind of place where you can find
someone just by going into the general store, or post office, and
asking for directions. That's how I found Rex Bundy.*

*The old-time ranch hand and rodeo cowboy settled in the
valley "before it was ruined." He has surrounded his house with
vegetable gardens, in the midst of suburbia. And he looks out
gloomily at his "unneighborly neighbors."*

*"Folks know me around here. Been here long 'nough," he
says. He isn't all that old, but he likes to think that he is. "Sel-
dom do you find a person my age around," he says, almost de-*

fiantly. "*They're few and far between. But I don't mean to move, or die. Too mean.*"

Maybe what makes him feel so old and belligerent is not just the way the valley has changed. But why. He laments the ending of the old communal ways of rural neighborliness, but he curses those whom he believes are responsible for its demise.

And Rex Bundy is a top hand when it comes to cursing.

Neighbors Used to Look Out for Each Other
Rex Bundy

Neighborliness, in the way it used to be here, you could trust anybody. Like they would throw away the keys when they built a house. They never took the locks. I know one hardware store where they never even sold locks. Same as you'd leave your car by the roadside. You come back two or three days later and someone would have come along and had a flat tire and they needed a spare tire and they'd take it, but they'd leave you a note. Same way with gasoline. They'd siphon gas out and leave a note.

I've seen that happen.

And it used to be you could go to town and put your groceries and stuff in your car and walk away and have a couple of beers and nothing would be touched at all. You could even leave your keys there in your car.

But you can't do things like that nowadays. Now you come back and they have all four wheels off and the transmission and half the motor is gone.

The neighborliness isn't there. It just isn't there. In those days neighbors used to look out for each other, but now it is as if they're looking for some way to cut your throat, to irritate you.

Maybe it's the people who've moved in here. City people. We got 'em living in here that commute to California, to work. One guy here he commutes to New York, to work. Yeah, by plane. I can't blame 'em for wanting to live in God's country, no, sir. But they are different kind of people.

They're used to the big city where they didn't know their

neighbors. They're used to a different style of life than we had. Maybe they lived next door to someone for ten, fifteen years, and they didn't know their names. And it wasn't like that here. You knew everyone within forty miles. And they knew you. So you couldn't steal from anyone.

Someone would ask you about so-and-so. And you'd say, I know him. He lives up such-and-such a creek.

And I don't know; the city people, they brought in city ways. Some of 'em are all right. But there's a sad lack of fellowship or something among 'em.

'Course, in those days, if you didn't like someone you just didn't associate at all with them. Now you don't have much of a choice. They're so many people out here in the Bitterroot Valley that they're in your backyard anyway.

Many times I have complained about the lack of courtesy nowadays. And a lack of neighborliness. It wasn't so bad until the new people moved in and we tried to be neighborly. They don't reciprocate. Seems like they have no consideration for others. Like it used to be.

Community life is shot. Because of these people don't visit. Even the older people don't visit like they used to. And you're sort of alone.

Well, you can lay a lot of that on transportation. It used to be you didn't travel far with a team of horses. And, I think, we slipped up someplace there.

The main trouble, I think, is chasing that almighty dollar. Maybe it's the quest for that almighty dollar that makes people that way. I don't know. For me, I am just contented if I have enough to pay the damned bills and get my wife and my daughter what they want. There are a lot of things I would like to have I haven't got. But, I got a place. I've got my garden. If I want to work, that's fine, and if I don't want to work, that's fine, too. And I like to set and talk.

But the new people, they don't act like that. They've got no time.

In the old days, fellows would get to town and they would talk the price of grain and the price of cattle. That was the way they found out about things, because there was a lack of communication, from outside. From the radio and all that. And so, when they did communicate, then it was in the sense of helping each other. If a fellow found out that a certain kind of wheat was good, he passed the word.

See, I was born and was raised in a little town. Everybody knew everybody. I could even tell you what color toilet paper they used. It was one of that kind of town. Four hundred and fifty people, or something. It's a little bigger, now. Some of the farmers and ranchers, they've moved into town, where they never lived before. And things changed.

We used to live at a slower pace. Not in such a big hurry. In those days, we had time to be neighborly.

The Gospel of Good Roads: A Letter to the American Farmer, *published in 1891 by the League of American Wheelmen, blamed the "decline of agriculture" on bad farm roads, which "were the worst in the world." No longer should farmers be responsible for maintaining these muddy roads, declared the new Gospel; rural roads should be the responsibility of the government and be paved with tax monies. After all, we no longer use a scythe and flail, and "have long since ceased to shoot crows with the old flintlock."*

Progress demanded paved roads. And that the government pave them.

On the new roads the rural people would be able to get to town faster, transport their crops more safely, and have more access to the benefits of the city. "To have a good road is to save, to accumulate, to improve and prosper," the new Gospel promised.

And it was all true enough. The new roads would forever change the way of life on farms and ranches.

But the roads went both ways. Not only did they bring the countryside into the city, they brought the city into the countryside. Rural people were to become more familiar with urban ways of living and thinking. And little by little rural life became more and more urbanized.

From the windows of their ranch houses through the years, five generations of Skinners have seen their world pass down the country road beyond their corrals. In the Jordan Valley of eastern Oregon change comes slowly. But it has come.

"Our way of life," Robert Skinner said, "has gone down that road."

The Process of Change
Robert Skinner, Jr.

The main road went right by here. Any of the neighbors who were headed for Jordan Valley, they would stop in to visit, they were expected to stop, and to eat dinner, if they came by at dinner. And if they came at night, they stayed the night. I don't remember the times when people *really* gathered in, but I do remember the last years of it.

Nowaday we are a much more mobile society than we were then. But then we had much more of a local community life.

Going to town? I was in the third grade before I ever saw a train. Before I ever got out of Jordan Valley. Nowaday these youngsters go to town many times a year. In those days we just stayed here. And on the ranch, here, it would sometimes be months before some people went to town. Some people didn't even go to Jordan Valley for years.

In those days they'd have dances and get-togethers in the big ranch house. My grandmother always had a crowd of the young folks around.

The country was in the process of change. But we didn't know it. So they'd have these parties and get-togethers maybe once every two weeks. In the wintertime most people weren't too busy. And so they'd just have a dance or an affair at someone's house. And they'd visit and entertain themselves and have potluck dinners and dance.

But I guess it got to be too much for the ladies. They progressed to where they would rent a hall. And those affairs were then held there.

And then the highways were put in. And people got to where they could go to someplace else. And that was the end of our get-togethers.

When the cars came in! And people could get out! And the highway had something to do with that all right! The process of change had begun before that. But that put the finishing touches on it.

So you see we went from those get-togethers in our home, that was a private affair, to a semiprivate affair in a hall, and from there it went out the window. After World War II we had a few of those get-togethers, but that didn't last for very long. Now we don't have any.

From what I can remember it probably was in World War II that the people changed. They were all rearranged.

Some people that were shipped out didn't come back and a lot of new people came in and a lot of the ranches changed hands because during the war you couldn't get help and they sold out and the ranches were combined. In this little valley we had at least three times the families then that we have now. They lived on smaller acreage. And the valley supported those people. They made a living. They lived, a lot of them, in one-room houses, big families, who now would be considered living on the poverty level, but most of them back then ate pretty good and the kids seemed to be happy.

But when those people got a taste of something different, in World War II, they weren't satisfied anymore. They sold out. They didn't come back.

On the new roads, or at least beside them, rode a host of unseen travelers, like silent ghosts. These were the spirits of those miracles, the telephone lines, the electric wire, the radio wave, and later the television picture, which spread from the cities, the spiderwebs of modern technology that brought urban fantasies to the quiet countryside.

And, like everyone else, the rural people were fascinated. Everyone had to buy one of these fantasies.

Most often people tend to forget that in many small ranching communities the electricity did not "come in" until the 1930s. And in many places there was no electricity until the late 1950s.

So these changes have been sudden. And recent. And dramatic.

In the little New Mexico village of San Cristobal the process of change has been much the same as in any other rural community. Maybe it seems clearer because the valley is smaller and everything that happens is so easily visible. The way Jenny Vincent has described it, it seems like a microcosm of what happened throughout the West.

"One morning, we woke up as usual, and it just seemed like our community's way of life had stopped," she said. "And another way of life began."

When Electricity Came In
Jenny Vincent

There was a road from way in the bottom of the valley all the way up to the ranch. But it was in pretty bad condition. It was partly the old wagon road from Taos to Questa and that part was in pretty good shape, but the road down below, in the valley, was bad. So we got together with some of the men in the community to talk about what could be done. We decided to rebuild the road.

Men loaned their wagons and their horses. They worked on the road when they were home. Everybody in the community, I think, worked on that road.

And we rebuilt it. Because if the community had a problem, in those days, we had to take care of it ourselves. No one was going to do it for us.

In those days there'd be a lot of helping each other. When haying time came our kids used to go down and help. When the hay was ready people would take turns and go from one place to another and everybody was pretty much working together on the haying.

People helped one another because they had to. It was that way in most every rural community.

The people in our valley were almost all Spanish-speaking. It wasn't a big valley. Maybe a few miles long and a mile wide in the foothills of the Sangre de Cristo Mountains. There were about twenty families in the valley. Just below Lobo Peak, Wolf Peak, which is fourteen thousand feet high.

Poor farm families . . .

On the farms in the valley it was subsistence farming. Everybody had cows and horses. They had milk. They had chickens. They had gardens. And for the most part people could get by on their own for food and meat.

Most of the men went off to Wyoming to herd sheep. To earn a little money. They herded big flocks in those days. Some of them went only at sheep-shearing time and then in the fall they went into the fields of the San Luis Valley, up in Colorado, harvesting potatoes, or they went picking peaches and apples on the western slope of the Rockies.

But the valley was home, for everyone. No one liked to leave it. They were independent-minded people and they didn't like working for anybody.

The town of Taos had maybe a few thousand people. But it was "the city" to the people in the valley. And so they didn't like their kids leaving the valley and going even to Taos and getting any highfalutin ideas, in "the city." There was a lot of anti-Taos feeling and there still is.

It was fifteen miles to "the city." And with a horse and wagon that was far, far away.

But after the war, pickup trucks began to take the place of the old horse and wagon. That was in the late forties. Men would send home their wages, during the war, and that would help their families economically in many ways. And people started to get pickup trucks.

The people could then go into Taos on a Saturday to do their marketing. Our local general store charged high prices. So people were happy to be able to go to town and do their groceries.

And then people learned how to go to banks. They hadn't known about banks. I remember we were surprised when we sold a piece of property on the ranch to the Medina family, and this was as late as in 1955, and they made a down payment in cash they had stashed away in a coffee can, in dollar bills, fives and

tens and maybe a few twenties. They made a one-thousand dollar
down payment like that, out of a coffee can.

Then, after the war, the first washing machines came into the
valley. First it was those old gasoline washing machines. But
when electricity came into the valley, in 1947, then everybody
started to get electric washing machines. Those electric washing
machines was one of the first things people got, to help the
women. They had big families.

Of course, then we had the electric lights. And soon after that
there was the television, and all the rest.

These things, the pickups and the electricity, they tied the people to the towns. After that, the people in the valley, the rural
people, couldn't be independent. Ever again.

*On no ranch in Montana do the natural grasses grow as
tall. The old buffalo grasses are waist high. Sometimes it is difficult to see the cows hidden under the growth of mountain weeds
and scrub trees. But, that's the way Boyd Charter wanted his
ranch to be, as much like the old days of the West as it could be.
"The way the Indians left it," Boyd used to say. And that's just
the way his wife, Anne, has kept it.*

*So naturally she's partial to the old ways of looking at things.
But she's no know-nothing environmentalist when it comes to
ranching. As a ranch wife, most of her life, she is a very down-
to-earth sort of lady.*

*Her opinion on what went wrong in ranching is historical and
practical. It seems to her, she says, that nowadays rural life is
wholly beholden to urban ways, urban needs, urban markets,
urban machinery, urban technology, and urban goals.*

*"And that," she says, "is our problem on the ranches. Rural
problems have become urban problems!"*

The Tide Turned
Anne Charter

And I have always said, When the ranchers have to live up to their city neighbors and have all the conveniences they are not going to make it. There was a time, before electricity came in, before refrigerators and all that, that we were able to make it. To live good. Without all that. And without too many hardships. Then after World War II, the electricity came in and every ranch had to have the electricity.

And at the time I said, There is something wrong.

And I still think it was then the tide turned. From that time on ranching as a way of life was done.

When people who lived on a ranch and raised families on a ranch, they had to compete with their city neighbors, why, they were never going to make it. It started with those kitchen and house gadgets, the washing machines and electric toasters.

Then it went to the big farm machinery and the artificial fertilizers and the stuff that's come in. One thing led to another. But it all started with the electricity. And the idea that on a ranch we had to have everything they had in the cities.

Once people on a ranch had to make-do with what they had. But when that electricity came in things changed. We had to have everything we couldn't ever make by ourselves.

And it has made it that everything we produce costs too much to produce. And everything we sell costs too much to sell. And everything we buy, all of those things made by electricity, costs too much for us to buy.

So, you see, life on a ranch has been urbanized; it is no longer really a rural way of life. The rancher, he is plugged into the electricity from the city.

In the Sweat of Thy Face Shalt Thou Eat Bread

5

The Cattle Was Just As Tough As We Was
Tug Pettit

And you could tell when there's going to be a norther' coming. See that white cloud over yonder. Well, down there in the plains there'd be a real blue light, on the horizon, almost black, when the norther' is coming. And you better have all your clothes you got on or it will freeze you right to death. So we'd saddle our horses, when we would see that, and get all our cattle, to bring them back up.

And we'd get out and holler in the wind for the cows, Yoo-ooh-ooh!

The plains was just as level as a board. You can come out of the road and go off across the plains as nice and as smooth as if you were still on the road. And the gamma grass was all nice and tall. But now it's all cotton fields and wheat fields. When you go east and south you get into broken country, a bit. That is more or less scrub trees. Mesquite. But on the plains it was all grasses.

Boy, you can see a cow a mile away or two. And if they can hear you hollering, away they come. It was all grassland and flatland.

And our stock it was all over the country. They drifted. So when the norther' would come the older boys would have to saddle up and bring them cows back. I can remember times when the snow was so deep your feet would drag in the snow on a good-sized horse.

In the summer the cattle stay in close because there is plenty of grass and water. But, in the winter, we had to begin fencing to hold them.

And we would put a drift fence in every fifty miles. That would hold back the snowdrifts a bit. But it wouldn't hold the cattle.

Cattle and horses, especially cattle, they'll go right ahead, facing into a storm, or rain. But they won't go sideways to 'em. Not too long. They'll go from it. And as long as they keep on traveling they stay warm. But if a drift fence, it stops 'em, and they don't turn back, why, they'll stomp each other down just climbing and pushing on that fence.

And they'll break the fence over and they'll go for another fifty miles. If the snow was too bad those cows they'd just drift together and break over the fences.

Those cattle were just as tough as we were. And meaner.

Pettit was in his late seventies, I think. He was not the sort of man whom you asked about his age.

He was sinewy, wiry, hard. And he had the look of a man who did not have to exercise to keep in shape. When I heard he and his wife were still ranching, for the fourth time, in California, I asked how he managed to keep going at his age. Oh, he said, I'm not the man I was when I'd been younger. I can't ride the way I used to, no more.

And I said, Now how's that?

And he said, Well, I saddle up and ride out just once a week these days. I ranch mostly by car. Not on horseback, the way I used to.

And I said, But you ride out once a week, at your age?

And he said, Yah, well, I ain't all that far gone, yet. I hope.

Lean of language, his words were clean as a dog's tooth. The tone was hard; it was that of a hard man who had had a hard life. And yet, he was matter-of-fact. Not boastful. That was Tug Pettit's way of laying back, of being cool, of keeping a low profile.

It was the ranchers' way of boasting, without boasting. Of immodest modesty. Of an ironic manner many westerners have of exaggerating their feats of manhood, by deprecating themselves.

One time, I remember, a fellow from a television station here in New Mexico was sent down to the state fairgrounds to inter-view a rodeo cowboy who had taken a bad spill. The television reporter asked the kind of question you'd expect him to ask: "How do you feel?" he said. And the rodeo cowboy gave the ex-pected answer. "Well," he said, "I guess I just about broke every bone in my body. One time or another. But they don't hurt me hardly, none."

That was a way of talking about things that Tug Pettit would have approved of. It was a fitting way of showing how tough things were in cowboying, by showing how tough you were, with-out being too forward.

"Shit!" replied Gerald Allen.

One of that independent breed of salty-tongued, eastern Ore-gon ranchers, Allen thought that kind of talk was romantic non-sense. He called it the "rodeo conception" of ranching. Though it might be all right for telling tall tales of the "good old days," or for showing off in the rodeo arena, it didn't help "one damned bit in branding a calf."

And yet, in his own way, Allen talked in the same way about his working on his ranch. Ranching wasn't "no sweet bed of roses," he said; "it was a bed of manure."

"But boasting about how tough it is," he boasted, "don't make it one damned bit easier."

On Horseback
Gerald Allen

In the old days, branding on horseback was the way it was done. Even today some fellows still do it that way, in their heads.

But I don't know about it.

That tradition thing on the work of working cattle on horse-back, there is a big difference of opinion on it. Such as branding in the old way.

But, shit, it's lots harder.

One time the calf is over there and then it's over here. And each time you got to go to the ground, with your iron. Then you got all the expenses of hauling horses up there to do the branding.

And you got to have one case of whiskey and two cases of beer up there for the buckaroos.

Now if I take one of those calf tables out there and I take one other man besides myself, we can do the same work as eight men on horseback can do. Each time the calf is there on the table, he's in the same place. And my vaccine gun and knife and iron is right up there. And you don't have to stoop over, or move around.

Now two men can go out, afoot, and work more cattle faster and be easier on the animal, and with more competency, all the way around, than you can do with eight buckaroos. Some of these things are just modern-day.

But if you try to get one of the same buckaroos to come and help you on the calf table you would insult the son of a bitch beyond repair. And you could never make amends to him in your whole lifetime.

The buckaroo, he has got a rodeo conception.

"Now, the difference between a rancher and a cow is that a cow's got four legs. . . ."

That wasn't the worst thing said about ranchers in the old days. A rancher might not have been thought to be as lowly as a cowboy, whom President Chester Arthur once likened to a bunch of "desperadoes," but if he was a notch higher on the social ladder, he was not thought of more highly by the leaders of society in the East.

Ranching in the homesteading days was very close to the earth. So was the rancher. In that time being down-to-earth was not necessarily a compliment.

Many of the pioneer ranchers had been dirt farmers. Before they became ennobled and bold homesteaders on the frontier they had merely been yeomen behind a plow in the quiet pasture of some little rural town. They were conservative and proper citizens who were not given to the daring deeds of bravado that ranchers were supposed to perform. And they were guided by

the puritanical codes of hard work and Christian morality. It was just as well, considering the labor required to build a ranch in the wilderness.

One of the chroniclers of ranching, "as it was, not as we think it was," is Omar S. Barker. He was too sick and old, he said, to tell me this tale of his family. So he gave me something that he had written about those days, so long ago that the paper was brown with the years and crumbled in my fingers.

Even so, Barker signed his letter that accompanied this reminiscence, much as he always did, Dios y Libertad, *God and Liberty. And beneath he scribbled his initials:*

"S.O.B."

We Didn't Ride Like Sure 'Nough Cowboys
Omar S. Barker

Some story-reading folks seem to have got the idea that everything in the West of from forty to eighty years ago was either big ranches or measly little damn-nester outfits, plowing up grass that God meant for cattle. Of course they're partly right but partly wrong too. My father never either owned or worked for a big cow outfit, but he certainly wasn't what anybody could rightly call a damn-nester.

To suck in a deep breath and round up the main facts in one big go-round, he was a stonemason preacher who sweated out a living for his big, hard-eating family by farming, hunting, running a sawmill, and raising cattle way up here in the rugged canyon of the New Mexico Rockies in the days when "horse power" meant something on four legs and the only vehicles in which to ride the twenty-five miles to town were a wagon, a buckboard, or a saddle.

On second breath let me add that Pa always managed to raise a few more cattle than kids, which made him a cowman at least in a small way. Highest tally of Texas-bred cattle running loose at any one time with the SLB brand on them was probably about 150. Not very many by cow ranch standards.

Most he-forked cowhands of trail and roundup would have

laughed at some of the ways we cow-worked that little bunch of wildish hornies up here in the timber. Some of them did sometimes poke a little fun at us younger buttons for the sweat-caked horsehair on our britches and the spraddle-legged way we walked after a day's riding on Beaver Creek and Lone Tree Mesa "lookin' after" the cattle. For there were never enough saddles to go around, and although straddling a pony bareback never seems so bad when you first start out, it sure does get you in the end.

Ma generally tried to make us rig up a "Mormon saddle" by lashing an old piece of quilt on the horse to sit on. But that was the way girls managed when they had to ride anywheres without saddles. My brother Marion and I acquired many a blister from the ridgepole of Old Slocum, or Old Prince, rather than risk being called sissies. If I had to ride far without a saddle today I'm afraid I'd hire a mattress.

What I really set out to tell about was the way we used to work this little bunch of cattle along the willow-clumped meadows of Beaver Creek, on steep mountain slopes, in thickets of aspens and scrub oaks, around the rims of limestone cliffs and through the forest primeval.

When we wanted to gather the cattle for a branding, to cut out a fat steer to butcher, to bring in another likely-uddered heifer for a milk cow, or just to tally a count, we didn't ride circle like sure 'nough cowboys do and drive them into a roundup.

Nossir, we "swooked" 'em! Maybe it was his vocal development from singing hymns, maybe it was a free-throated vigor he had brought with him all the way from his native Virginia mountains (Pa was what folks sometimes referred to as a jackleg preacher), but wherever he got it, Pa had the farthest carrying voice for calling cattle that ever brought an old she-longhorn out of the timber.

Here's the way it worked: Range cattle, especially on juicy mountain grass, get hungry for salt. Instead of leaving it out for them to eat whenever they wanted it, at fairly frequent intervals we "hand-salted" them. That is, we called the cattle, then put handfuls of coarse stock salt on the ground for them to lick. If they didn't come when we called, they got no salt. You'd be surprised how quickly they learned. Young calves following their mothers automatically learned as they grew up. Usually to gather practically all his cattle, all Pa had to do was to call them. The reason we called it "swooking" was simply that "swook" is the approximate sound of the call—but loud.

Whether they would have come as well for any other sound I don't know, but Pa's sonorous, long-drawn *"swoo-oo-ook"* would bring the cattle racing down the mountain from as far away as they could hear him, which was sometimes three miles in the clear mountain air.

Even when we drove in to the ranch for a branding, or for winter feed, someone rode ahead to beat the band. This was certainly not cowboy style, but it made the job of shoving the drags through knee-punishing timber a mighty lot easier. Often Ma or one of the older girls sounded off in the lead while us boys, or Pa, did the driving.

It wasn't by any means cowpunching big-ranch style, but it wasn't damn-nestering either. As we grew up and saw something of sure 'nough cow work on the big ranches out among the foothills and mesas, our own little cow work up here in the timber seemed to us mighty crude and awkward and puny and tame—and I reckon it was.

But, looking back on it now, I think we kinda liked it.

On the ranch of the Skinner family with its modern machinery, the corrals are built in the same way they have always been. Bundles of reeds and thin branches are tied together and are placed between two rows of fence posts, to cushion the horses and cows. They make resilient and strong corral fences that have been built in the same way for generations.

Even the fence posts, some of them, were fifty years old. And Robert Skinner touched them with affection.

It was a little like hanging the old saddles up in the barn. And keeping them as a living memory. But the corral fences were more than that. They were memories that were still in use.

The Skinners, grandfather and father, remembered the old ways of ranching with bittersweet memories. For what they re-

called was a way of life which had shaped their lives. And those tough memories had hardened them into the sort of men they were today.

Nothing Was Easy Then
Robert Skinner, Jr., and Robert Skinner, Sr.

FATHER: And working with cattle, that would be one of the things that I remember as a boy. If you like outdoors and if you like working with animals, ranching is the way to do it. We don't feel the need for backpacking and those recreational activities so many people are after now, because we get that in our everyday work.

But it is still hard work. Ranching will always be hard work.

And horseback riding, we looked at that as a chore more than a recreation. But that's what we liked to do. So horseback riding and working cattle, that may be recreation in a way.

GRANDFATHER: One memory I have of wintertimes is that it seems like winters were harder then. And colder. So it was harder working cattle. It seems like we always had more snow on the ground. And it was harder to get around. And it got forty below.

So even horses couldn't go through, sometimes.

FATHER: And I remember getting in those cold sheets at night in an unheated ranch house.

And carrying wood for that darn kitchen stove. They'd cut sagebrush for an hour or two every afternoon. And we would have to haul it to the house. Every day. Every day in the fall we hauled huge wagons of that sagebrush into the house, from out where that airplane hangar is now.

Nothing was easy then.

GRANDFATHER: Even what you would call recreation was hard work. It would surprise you some of the things that we did for recreation.

On this rock hill we have here in wintertime we would go down this hill on a piece of iron sheet. Like sleighs. And we would "ski" on those rocks, on pieces of barrel staves, when it snowed, not even tying them on, you know, or anything like that.

FATHER: And in some ways, working cattle was easier than having fun.

GRANDFATHER: But, you know, in those days we played hard. We worked hard. We did everything hard. It was our way, our way of life.

The ranch was set in the grasses of the foothills. Beyond its trees the mountains rose majestically. "Majestic" is the only word to describe their surprisingly grave and stark contours; an awesome sight. From the ranch house the highest ridges and peaks could be seen as clearly as if they were within reach of your hand. Some old-timers said that on a clear day, in the mountains, a man could almost see heaven.

Beautiful as it was, it was hard country. The rangeland was so poor and sparse it took one hundred acres to feed one cow. And to the south, in the desert flats of Alamogordo, there was hardly enough grass on one section, that is 640 acres, for five cows, said one local rancher, Billy Stephenson. "That's what I call real hard *country," he said.*

Stephenson's I–X Ranch was located inbetween the Sacramento Mountains and the lava fields of the desert, which was known as the Jornada del Muerto, *the Journey of Death. It was a lonely and isolated place.*

The town of Oscuro, down the road, consisted of three buildings, all of them abandoned. Down the other way the nearest town was twenty-five miles away; it was Carrizozo, the big town, thereabouts, which had been pretty quiet since the day Billy the Kid rode through. Most of its buildings seemed boarded up and left to rot into history. All day that I was in town the sand from the desert blew down Main Street. No one noticed.

And yet, in the midst of the "real hard country," Billy Stephenson's I–X Ranch was set like a jewel in its beautiful surroundings, for he had built it mostly with his own loving hands, from the one-room log cabin it once had been; it was comfortable and as esthetically pleasing as any home I have ever been in; in spite of the "real hard country."

"Mostly in this deserty country, you got to work for what you get, hard," he said.

But I Don't Mind Working
Billy Stephenson

In the last fifteen years I don't think I been off of this ranch more than four days. Oh, I did take off a week when I got married. That was fifteen years ago. And I haven't been off this ranch since then, more than two days at a time. As far as being able to take off and enjoy a two-week vacation, I never done it in my life. The way the help situation is, I can't afford to have enough men working, where I can take off.

Sure can't go off and leave it for a very long time.

But I don't mind working. When you are working cattle sometimes you are working fourteen hours a day. It really doesn't bother me. Because I am just as happy working on the ranch as I would be going to New York.

I stay at home because I got more to do than what I can. You got seventy-five or eighty miles of fence you got to keep up. And you can always go out and find a windmill that's probably broke down, or a drinking tub for the cattle that has broke down, or is ready to break down, or a pipeline that can break down at any time, or if you don't check your reservoirs then you can lose a reservoir full of water. And you will have a lot of thirsty cows.

And there are all the vehicles you have around here; if any work has to be done on them, we do it ourselves. In the wintertime when the weather is too bad to get out in the pasture we are down there in the garage overhauling an engine, or repairing something. There is always something that needs to be fixed. There's always something that is tearing up.

I think it's a lot worse now than it was fifty years ago. Because back then you didn't have all of these mechanical things that we have now. We got tractors and pump-jack engines and no counting how many mechanical things. And most of them you use only once, and they break down.

I think we spend more time working on mechanical things and

vehicles than we do going out there on horseback. Except for the fall and spring of the year, now we spend very little time on horseback. For the rest of the time we're out running around in the pickups.

And where you used to have half a dozen men working on a ranch you got one or two, now, and without all these mechanical things you couldn't operate a ranch. Even with an extra man.

So it goes round in circles.

But I don't know if that's being independent or individual. It's just something we do and we take for granted and we don't think about it.

If something breaks down we just go fix it. There is nobody to call to do it. And when you do something out here you know it's something that benefits you.

And so, it's hard to explain to anyone what working on a ranch is really like. It's something you do. By yourself, mostly. You can make it sound good or you can make it sound bad. You can paint any picture of it you want to, I guess.

Me, I stay in ranching because it's something I like to do. And always have. I grew up on a ranch and it's just something that you get to like. You know, after you go someplace else and see how different people live in different places, you just want to come back even that much more. You are glad you are a rancher.

Ranching, for me, is the only thing I have ever done.

One eastern traveler wrote of the ranchers and cowboys he met on a tour of the great West, in the 1880s: A man in the West "may be as proud as Lucifer, but necessity arrays him in a homely dress; and he appears humble." But, don't be fooled, the traveler said, for his modest appearance is deceiving: "Though he looks like a shack," the rancher "may be a millionaire" beneath his shabby clothes. And he may be arrogant as Hell itself.

That hasn't changed much.

Some ranchers go to great lengths to hide their opinions. And to seem to be modest, even ignorant, in public. That may be because so much of what they have to say is fundamentally at odds with, and highly critical of, the way of living of the rest of the country. And beneath their politeness there is often a deep anger, ironic and caustic, about how the country sees their way of life.

One rancher who had no such modesty, false or otherwise, was the Montana cattleman, Wallace McRae, of the Rocker Six Ranch; he was "as opinionated as a preacher," they said, "and about twice as moralistic." As a poet, both privately and publicly, he has written and spoken to whomever would listen about what he called "the stereotypes and hypocrisies" in the way the country sees ranching and ranchers see themselves.

McRae was more than blunt; he was sometimes cruelly honest. But, as he said, "The truth isn't easy to take."

My Philosophy in Running a Cow Outfit
Wallace McRae

My philosophy in running this cow outfit is let the cows run themselves as much as possible. That's the trouble with crops. You see, you don't let crops go do their own thing. You got to watch crops, all the time. But you can let your cows do their own thing. And, perhaps, the more you let a cow do her own thing, the better she's going to do.

So part of my philosophy and lots of ranchers like me is: Let a sick cow die!

And why do I think like that? Because I will be rid of the sick cow and I will be rid of her offspring. I won't never be tempted in the fall to save any sickly replacement heifer out of her, or to go sell a sick cow.

That's half of what is wrong with the cow business right now. We've been so careful with these cattle that we haven't let natural selection take its place. And when you get in an economic crunch it behooves you to take better and better care of these cattle; to ride them more and more and go around with a syringe in your hip pocket.

So you get weaker cows. Not stronger cows.

Of course, I could be out there today poking around with those cows of mine. And I'm sure there's some cow out there with lump jaw, or foot rot, or with a spoiled bag. If I was one hundred percent efficient I would be out there worrying and solving those things.

Economics of the cow business forces you to do that. But if you can resist that, you are going to end up with a whole lot cleaner and healthier cows. And a lot better meat.

But, my philosophy won't let me do that. Maybe I'm just perverse. Though I know lots of ranchers who think the way that I do.

One neighbor of ours, an excellent rancher, who is one of the most perverse people I know, he really knew how to run a ranch but he refused to run it the way you're supposed to because that's the way you *were supposed to.*

And he used to tell this story of a college graduate who came and tried to sell him on hiring him on as a consultant. This fellow told him: I can help you run a whole lot better outfit than you're running, right now. You just hire me. And I can show you how to run this place at least twice as good.

And our neighbor said, Well, yeah! But the only thing wrong with that is I am only running this outfit half as good as I know how to, right now!

He told it as a joke. But that was kind of his basic philosophy to run that outfit half as good as he could.

And I think a lot of us ranchers do that. That's how we think. Because if we were running these outfits as well as we knew how we'd have to use a whole lot more energy, and be more capital-intensive than we are right now. But ranching would not be the same.

I can look at my range and visualize double the carrying capacity of cows. Just like that. Netting more money in the long run.

But I don't want to do that.

Maybe I just don't want to get that management-intensive. Maybe I don't have the ability. I know that I just don't have the inclination.

Maybe driving a new car and being seen in the right circles is becoming important to some ranchers. They forget all they got comes from a cow. I don't know. But it's hard for me to understand ranchers who feel like that.

Maybe I'm a masochist. Maybe we all just like to suffer.

The land is the friend and adversary of the rancher. And while he knows he cannot live without it, there are times when he cannot live with it; it is yielding and unyielding, forgiving and unforgiving.

Sometimes the rancher may feel a warmth toward the land, as though it was part of his family, the source of his being, as much as his parents and grandparents, the place of his roots. Then, there are times when it seems his sworn enemy, determined to kill him.

On the rangeland of the mountains and plains of the West the land is hard. Mostly semiarid. In the honest days before the real estate speculators changed its name, as if a pariah, the entire West was known as "The Great American Desert." No matter what it is called, it still is; from Montana to New Mexico the rainfall is rarely more than thirteen inches yearly, and often is less.

Still, that very hardness and stubbornness of the land has created a strong if begrudging bond between those who ranch on it and its "damned orneriness." It may be that the bond is strengthened, not in spite of, but because of this.

In the dry and stark desert flats and desert hills of cactus on the Hills' ranch in southern New Mexico, this love-and-hate relationship is the way of life. That their ranch headquarters is set in a ghost town is somehow fitting. And the fierce defense of their land by Rita and Janaloo Hill has taken on the characteristics of the land itself.

They differ from other ranchers, if they do, only in the intensity of their angers.

The Land
Rita and Janaloo Hill

JANALOO: A sense of having your own place in the world; it gives one roots to have a piece of land.

RITA: People in the East, they have to be educated about the land. It belongs to everybody. But who takes care of it? The rancher. And yet, in the East, the people are given to think the rancher is the one who is exploiting it.

The land has only one real guardian. And that's the rancher.

If a rancher isn't an environmentalist he should get out of this business. Well, he's got to get out. He'll be out anyhow.

The ranching, at least the grazing of cattle, doesn't harm the land the way other things do. I think tests prove that a limited amount of grazing improves the grasses. Cattle trample the seeds into the soil. And they have proven that land the cattle were on and land right next door that was left vacant, well, the land the cattle were on has better vegetation.

And they say we ranchers are overgrazing the land. But I maintain that no one ever overgrazes. The Indians used to burn off the grass so that it would come back better. So it isn't the overgrazing that harms the land. If you put a bunch too many cattle on the land, well, they may trample it with their sharp hoofs, but that isn't overgrazing.

Besides, if the grass gets too short, a cow can't get at it anyway. A cow has only one set of teeth. So overgrazing, that's a silly word in the first place.

JANALOO: A well-conducted ranching operation does less damage to the environment than any other. I have always said that. Now, that's been proven.

RITA: The first stagecoach that come across this part of the country, they'd seen just one rabbit between Las Cruces, New Mexico, and Arizona. I read that. That's a historical fact. That's all the wildlife there was. By the rivers there was more. But down here in the desert where there was very little water there was very little wildlife. We all know that.

And it is the ranchers who water the wildlife. On most ranches what would wildlife do, if it wasn't for us ranchers? And our windmills?

JANALOO: Many of the old-time ranchers, they were exploitive. They thought the land was limitless and the resources were limitless. That's how the land got grazed off. And back in the 1890s there was this newspaper that said the land was all grazed off so it's time to move on.

RITA: It was what you call the pioneer mentality. There was just so much of the land, you could waste it and tear it up. And many of your urban people have the same silly, stupid idea. One would like to place each of them on half an acre and make them stay there. And live on that.

For the town person, the land is out there somewhere. The land's something that you turn your car around in and dump your trash in and all of that stuff. There is just endless land. So it doesn't matter. You see, for the town person, he has now got the pioneer mentality about the land. For the town person the land is there just to be wasted. And then you move on.

Those people are like locusts. Coming in and coming in. When a man builds his house out on the edge of town so he can be away from people, he takes the vegetation away from all the little creatures, the gophers and the rats and the ranchers and the cattle. So that they have to crowd onto some other land and go destroy that. Everybody kills the coyotes and the bobcats, but what about the suburbanites, who are looking for nature?

Here there is land with the nicest grass on it. Gamma grass. And those town persons, they have made a racetrack of the land with the cars, those four-wheel toys, looking for nature, until it's just a barren bunch of rocks and dirt. Ranchers, we don't do that. And if we try to stop them, the rancher has no power. This land of ours belongs to everybody; why should they be allowed to destroy it?

And the rancher is supposed to sit quietly and not get too gray-haired while the town persons tear over the hills, and those advertising agencies advertise that a car will go anywhere there's a road, or not.

I have some bumper stickers we've put on our cars: ONLY VANDALS DRIVE OFF ROADS and TRASHY PEOPLE DUMP TRASH. Now, I like that. Don't you?

Even so, I don't see how this land is going to survive for livestock or for wildlife or for ranchers or for anything else. No, I don't think it can. We don't have much faith, out here, in humanity anymore. I think animals are more honest, I really do, than people.

JANALOO: At least they're honestly selfish. They don't try to justify themselves with high-sounding words.

RITA· I think it would be right to make the rancher, or whoever lives on this land, responsible for the land. And make the rancher responsible for the grazing. And let the rancher keep the destroyers of the land off the land.

And if some of these destroyers of the land need hanging, bring them here to our ranch. Ten or eleven men were hanged here in the old days. And it is a nice, neat, quiet way to get rid of somebody who is destroying America.

So the prophets spoke:

"Thou shalt cherish thy pasture not only as a contributor to thy bank account but as a place of beauty for the delectation of thy soul, cultivating the friendship of the grasses," read the nineteenth of the Twenty Commandments for Grass Men, *written by Nebraska's prophets of natural grasses, Alice and Jim Wilson. In their celebration of the native range,* Grasslands, *they prophesied a return to the "Age of Grass" for without grass there can be no life on the semiarid lands of the West.*

Maybe that was what cattleman Wallace McRae meant when he said to me, "I don't raise cattle. I raise grass."

"In my grass," McRae said, "there is as much needed energy as there is energy in the coal beneath it. And the energy in my grass is renewable. Besides, we all eat grass, in the form of beef, and there is no way we can eat coal."

On her ranch of native rangeland grasses in the deep hills north of the Wyoming line, near Decker, Montana, Ellen Cotton voiced similar thoughts. She too spoke of the grass in an almost biblical, and yet practical, sense.

"Hereabouts, it's the grass that determines everything," she said.

The Grass
Ellen Cotton

One year a fellow from Soil Conservation came out here and he said to me, You haven't got a cattle ranch out here.

And I said, The heck!

And he said, No. You got a grass ranch out here.

And I said, I'll have to think about that. And I thought about it for a while.

And he said, If you don't exploit the grass it will go on for years.

And I said, That's very true.

And he said, I think you should try not to graze more than fifty percent of your grass in any one year. Because when you do that you may be depleting it. And if you keep on doing it then it wouldn't be able to sustain itself, like it has always done.

So I have always tried very hard not to overgraze the ranch. Though it is hard to do because livestock always will graze more in some places than on other places.

The grasses out here are a very, very valuable thing. More and more of our agricultural land is being torn up for cities and things. So our grass out here is like a national historical site. And it should be valued for what it is. Since the population in this country is still growing, we may reach a point where there isn't enough for cattle or enough for everybody to eat. And I think that we better start thinking about our grass and treasuring it.

When the snows come in the winter the grass holds it. The grass keeps that snow from blowing away.

And the old grass that gets laid down by the snow goes into the earth as a nutrient. It gets returned to the earth.

Now we can't go on and on taking and taking from the earth and not giving anything back. And we have to stop putting those artificial things back in the earth. We have to put those natural things back in the earth.

The way the grass does.

"Mr. Conservation," some have called him. And he is.

Ranchers are not often called that. Not homesteaders. But then, there have not been too many government conservation officials who have been working ranchers. One of the few men who "wore both hats," as he has said, is Elliott S. Barker. Born into a family of homesteading ranchers, in 1886, he became one of the oldest conservationists of grazing lands and wildlife in the American West.

On his family ranch he was taught to be a conservationist almost as soon as he was taught to shoot, he said. He remembered it clearly. It was one of the most important lessons of his life.

Metamorphosis from Rancher
to Conservationist
Elliott Barker

My metamorphosis from ranching to conservationist? I was a rancher, yes. And I learned early to hunt and fish. When I was eight or nine. In the early days we used quite a lot of game for food. Meat. But my mother didn't allow us to kill anything we didn't need that wasn't good to use. And that made a deadline on hunting from the first of March up into September that we couldn't kill a deer.

Well, it was kinda born in us to respect wildlife, for food.

And we early learned, when we was kids, through my mother more than anyone else, to be wildlife conservationists. Through my sister, too.

I remember when I was about eight or nine. My sister and her husband lived in a cabin, up the canyon. There was a good little trout stream there, that nobody ever fished. And I stayed with her for about a week when her husband was away on some chore of some kind.

One day she asked me to go down the creek and I remember her words well. She said, Catch us a mess of fish!

I caught some grasshoppers. And rigged up a willow pole. Then, I went down the creek and gosh darn, every pool you'd sneak up to and drop your line in you'd get a fish. And I caught "a mess of fish." I got too damn many. There was two strings of maybe thirty, forty trout. Nice trout.

Well, I went back up to the house. My sister, she didn't scold me. She called me over to her knee where she was sewing, or something, and she tried to explain how God had put those fish there for people to use. But not to waste! And here, she said, you got more than we can use. And she made me see it that way. And she gave me a good talking to.

And that impressed me with the seed of conservation at a very early age.

No man had witnessed more changes in the nation's laws and attitudes toward conservation. There was no man alive who had contributed as many years to the history of conservation. From the time, back in 1909, when he joined the Forest Service as a wilderness trail guide, until the time in 1950, when he came to symbolize wilderness preservation.

"This has been my life's work," he said. "And I'm a bit proud of it."

Seventy years of dedication to the preservation of the American West have seen Barker not only endorse but help to write many of the country's conservation laws. One of these is Regulation Three, of the U.S. Bureau of Reclamation—a fundamental law protecting wildlife on federal lands. Barker said simply, "I wrote that."

In his long lifetime, Barker has served as a game preserve manager, as a state game warden, as president, for three terms, of the Western Association of State Game and Fish Commissioners, and as president of the International Association of Game, Fish and Conservation Commissioners. He was, as well, a founder and first board member of the National Wildlife Federation. And one of the conservation acts he sponsored and helped persuade the Congress to enact was the Wilderness Preservation bill.

The awards for wilderness preservation, the protection of wildlife, range management and simple love of the West, which he has received, line two walls of his den. There are few honors that an environmentalist can be awarded that he has not been given.

Still, he began as a rancher's son, and became a rancher himself, and if he had his "druthers" he would be a rancher still. There is, in his mind, no contradiction between his two lives.

And with that in mind his opinion of the role of ranchers in the conservation of the West may be of more than rhetorical interest. "Ranchers have to be conservationists if they are to survive," he said matter-of-factly. "I learned that as a young'un."

On the morning that Elliott Barker and I talked of these things he had just celebrated his ninety-second birthday.

Ranchers Love the Land
Elliott Barker

All ranchers, they love the land. It is that "Home on the Range" idea. Most ranchers, I think, feel in that way. And most of them have been pretty good conservationists. On the eastern plains of New Mexico at least seventy-five percent of them were excellent wildlife conservationists. But, there's too many of them that have overgrazed and still overgraze their country. They think they're conservationists, but they don't practice it. Though a lot of them have woke up to it nowadays.

For the most part, the old ranchers have done the right thing by wildlife.

One time we didn't have one elk in the state of New Mexico. And about 1911, no, about 1906, one big rancher he began to stock elk there on his place. He went to great expense to do it. He·set aside two square miles of pasture with an elk-proof fence to keep the elk in there, to get them located, till the progeny felt that was home. He began with nine head and they scattered by the hundreds all over the northeast part of the state.

And down at Tatum, there was a rancher was a good friend of mine. On his place he had deer, sandhill deer. And he really took care of them. He had plenty of 'em. Then one year he put in a little herd of buffalo. Not to do anything with them commercially, or any other way, but because he wanted some buffalo out there on the range. Just because he liked them.

And he told me, That's where they were originally.

Well, he got them located and kept his herd down to twenty-five, thirty head. And he treated them just like his cattle. He sure was proud of those buffalo.

One time he said when they first settled there, they had lots of prairie chickens. And though he didn't overgraze his cattle, his cattle did cut down on the high forage. The prairie chickens, they became pretty scarce. Besides, they killed a lot of prairie chickens for winter food. Dressed them and hung them up in the back of the barn for shade. They'd freeze and keep all winter. That winter we killed eighty-nine prairie chickens, he said. He wasn't proud of it, but he said, In those days there were lots of prairie chickens and few of us.

Maybe that's why he wanted to preserve those buffalo!

And then there was the old Flying H Ranch, about seventy miles west of Roswell, where the owner, he was not much of a wildlife man. Not against them. And not particularly for them. But he liked his antelope. It was good antelope country. And he got to watching those antelope and they were getting to be very, very few. So he made a little survey of his ranch, the 122 sections of it, about 78,000 acres, with the help of his cowboys, and he came up with twenty-two head of antelope, all that was left.

And this story comes to me pretty straight. He called his cowboys and herders all in and told them: From this day on nobody on this ranch kills an antelope! None of you are to allow any outsider to come in! Put them off the ranch! If they come to hunt don't let them hunt! And if you have to use physical force, kick them off with blank shots! We are not going to kill any more antelope! That was back in the twenties. By 1937 they got too many antelope. They had over twelve hundreds, from the twenty-two head.

Now, that was a rancher that did that!

And then there was the old GS Ranch, north of Silver City. Back in 1926 they got forty-two head of elk. They went to the expense of building a 5,000-acre pasture for those elk, with an elk-proof fence, a heavy wire, six-inch mesh, and seven-foot-high fence. They didn't allow any killing. They let the elk increase and increase. When I came in as the state game warden, in 1931, the elk herd there was sacred, as far as everybody was concerned. The rancher helped persuade the U.S. Forest Service to let the elk into the Gila wilderness; they just didn't much want to do that. But he told them: We want to do that for the good of the country.

Not every one of the big ranchers were that big-hearted. A lot of them sure weren't. But the big ranchers, in my experience, for the most part were conservationists, at heart.

Our big conservation problem, our big problem, and it was really heartbreaking, was these homesteaders who came in in the twenties and thirties. That Depression came on. Times were really hard. And they were pretty well living off of game. Well, how the heck could you tell them not to?

If you prosecuted them, they didn't have money to pay a fine. They'd have to go to jail for a day for every dollar of the fine. If you did that the family was in harder shape than they was before. And there was no welfare then, as such.

Sometimes we had to shut our eyes to a situation that we couldn't remedy by doing what the law said. It was a poverty situation and a starvation problem.

Conservation, you know, that includes people, too.

Sisters of Ruth, and Other Ranch Women

6

Mothers and Daughters
Roberta Cheney

My grandmother was surely one of the strongest
people I ever knew. She was the midwife and nurse for all the
people in this valley. By herself, she delivered fifty-one babies.
She said that fifty was enough. Then a man came to her and he
said his wife was in labor and she should come. So she went to
the house and she delivered the baby. And she said that would
be the last delivery she made.

But then the woman had twins. And so it was fifty-one.

Coming to this valley, my grandparents were the first settlers.
They settled when there were no other white people here. They
had many Indian neighbors. In those days they lived very close
to the soil. And they did many of those things that all pioneer
people did—raising and preserving food and trying to live from
the land.

But my grandmother had grown up in the West. She was
born in Montana, a daughter of covered-wagon pioneers who
had come out in the gold-rush days. And so becoming a pioneer
again was nothing that was a bother to her.

My grandfather was strong too. He was one of those stern
Englishmen. Said grace at every meal. He always said that you
would choke on food if you took a bite before grace was said.
But it was really my grandmother, I think, who held the family
together. And the whole community depended on her.

There is a strong line of women in our family. Yes, I think

there is. Maybe because we have all of us sought fulfillment in our lives, in our communities, in our careers. So maybe having fulfilled ourselves in these ways, we don't have to keep searching for something to do, searching for ourselves.

But I was of that generation that thought ranching was not very exciting, and certainly not very honorable. And I was always embarrassed when I was asked, "What does your father do?" and I had to write down that he was a rancher. Though I thought rancher sounded a little better than farmer. So I always wrote down rancher.

And I was always sort of embarrassed about bringing people home. Because my father wore overalls.

My mother went to college in Bozeman [Montana]. And came back to the ranch. But I never felt my mother was at all happy in doing that. Every time my parents got a little money they bought another piece of land. Or they bought ten more cows. And I always thought my mother sort of resented that. Her living here. She was a very quiet person and never said anything. And she wasn't nearly the pioneering leader that my grandmother was. But she was determined that I would go to college, so that I would have a chance to choose my way of life.

She would say, I am nothing but a farmer's wife.

And that's the kind of attitude I grew up with, a little bit. That being a farmer was pretty low class.

So I was determined to go to college. I was determined to have a profession. It took me a long time to see the value of our land. Of coming back. Now, I do. Now, I feel very comfortable about being an educated person. Here. Whatever that means.

My children, the next generation, have a very different attitude. They are very interested in a more earthy existence and going back to the land. Of all the places in the world they come here to the ranch, because they like it best. And they have all traveled, they are all educated. Our daughter Karen is in the fields of the arts, drama, dance, ballet. Our daughter Maureen is very much a scholar. She is a medievalist, in French literature, and she is the head of her university department. But their greatest happiness is to come back here. To the ranch. And grow a garden and cut wood and build a fire in the fireplace and to render lard and to make homemade soap.

I find a great trend back to those things that their grandparents did. And that I resented and rejected.

And my grandchildren, who are fifth generation on this particular place, are even more so concerned with the land. What we can raise. What we can grow. How we can save the land.

I see an encouraging trend in my children and grandchildren. And in young people everywhere. That the basic things in life are not always money-making sort of things. That the good things are not always a big house in town. That family unity, a solid family connection, is most important. That if you can live a little nearer the land than most people do, you can have a happier life. That money is far less important than it was a generation ago.

And certainly the cities are less attractive and less important to young people than they were a generation ago. I see a return to basic living. To basic values. To really good values. Not so much the artificial things. And that is very encouraging to me.

My daughters have taught me many things. So many things. The times come when the children will teach their parents, if their parents can learn.

The more I look into it the more women in the West I find who deserve to be remembered, honored, written about. Not the Annie Oakleys and the Calamity Janes. The ordinary women.

Either women in the West are depicted as dance-hall girls, or the wife of an army officer, or "the Lady from Philadelphia," who no matter what happens always remains pure. That's foolishness. Maybe it is time to remember the women who really made the West. And I do think that "made" is a good word to use.

By made, I mean the women who made the West human, who not only had, but led, the families, who advanced education, who made life stable.

The ranching women.

I don't think the West was made at all by the sheriff and those people. The women made the West.

On the tree-lined square where the county courthouse stands guard on the morality of the town, there is often a statue of the Madonna of the Trail. Many western towns revere that sculptured pioneer woman, the long-suffering, forever enduring mother of a brood of children who cling to her skirt as she trudges westward, through the mountains and deserts, conquering the wilderness while cradling an infant in one arm and a rifle in the other, until she discovers a peaceful homestead where she settles down to prepare dinner for her family. The perfect homemaker.

The noble woman of that stereotyped statue in no way resembled any of the pioneer women in Roberta Cheney's family. Not as she remembered them.

As a college teacher and a writer, she herself may have been a more realistic image of an old homesteading woman of the West. From their earliest beginnings these women were many times educated, independent-minded and self-reliant. They had to be to survive.

Even in retirement Roberta Cheney was like that. On her last Christmas card she was shown on horseback, her whitening hair tucked under her cowboy hat.

It was an old familial tradition, she said, for western women to do "their own thing."

Of the nearly 125,000 white women of the West who were working for a living, in the 1890 census, almost forty-five percent were domestic servants, seamstresses, and laundresses. But fifteen percent of them were professional women.

Though barely four percent of the nation's women lived west of the Mississippi, they comprised fourteen percent of the nation's women lawyers, ten percent of the women doctors, fifteen percent of the women writers and scientists, eleven percent of the women artists, ten percent of the women journalists and five percent of the women college professors. In all there were nearly 20,000 women professionals on the frontier.

Statues to such western women have yet to be erected on town squares. Nor do film and television westerns appear aware of their existence.

And yet, much of the exaggerated respect shown by cowhands for western women may have been partly due to the intellectual attainment of so many of them. To the unlettered ranchers and farmers that might have been a bit intimidating.

The English novelist Anthony Trollope, on his tour of the West in 1862, was impressed by the intelligence and independence of these women; but as he said, he wouldn't want to marry one. "I cannot fancy myself much in love with a western lady," he wrote; "they are sharp as nails, but then they are also as hard." Even worse: "They never practice the virtue of obedience" to their men, but believe "that destiny is to be worked out by the spirit and talent of the young women." And "they know so much more than they ought to."

If Eve had been a ranch woman, said Trollope, she would have never tempted Adam with an apple. She "would have ordered him to make his [own] meal."

On a ranch, in the early days, there had been "little division of labor" between men and women, as historian Ray Allen Billington noted in his America's Frontier Heritage, *for these ranch women "normally performed many of the tasks essential to frontier life." Men and women lived in "a fellowship of labor," wrote Ernest Groves, in* The American Woman, *and the women "could do the same things that men had been accustomed to doing." And such a pioneer woman was "characteristically self-reliant and self-expressive." She "shared the feeling of men."*

That was certainly true of Anne Charter. She came from a wealthy school in the East to marry the son of a famous outlaw. Her family was hardly enthusiastic. As far as her schoolmates and relatives were concerned, she might as well have gone to Morocco as to Montana. An aunt who had married a banker did write to say she admired her. But that was all.

But she was about as independent as any pioneer woman. She learned to be a rancher, and a good one.

"And my aunt, the one who married the banker, after they retired from London and Paris and all that, wrote a letter saying she had always wanted to do what I had done." She laughed. "But she never had the courage.

"Mostly they thought I'd lost my mind," she said.

The Reality of the West
Was Better Than the Dream
Anne Charter

When I was a young girl we lived in one of the new, fancy suburbs of St. Louis, Missouri. My family had to "keep up the standards." They were well-to-do. One of my aunts married a director of the Morgan Bank in western Europe. It was that kind of a family. And I went through all the things I was supposed to as a city-bred gal; I was sent all over the country and the world.

And then I married a cowboy!

I came from the city. City-bred. But my heart was always in the country.

And I had a sister, an older sister, who had moved west to a big, wealthy ranch outside of Sheridan, Wyoming, on the Bighorn River. One of the biggest and fanciest ranches out there. My brother and I, we went out to visit them. And I thought that the West would be pretty glamorous, but it was pure dude.

One summer of discontent, when I was looking for further horizons, there was a party on that ranch. And there was a man who had bought the McCormack Ranch up the river outside of Jackson Hole and he decided he would try to run it as a dude ranch.

Well, I had never met him before that evening. But I told him, You can't run a dude ranch unless you had some female help. I didn't know very much about cooking, but I volunteered to run the kitchen.

So we went out there. And I sent home for a cookbook.

That was a beautifully and delightfully informal summer. We had about thirty dudes but we really didn't care what happened. We just had a riotous time. We were so young.

Boyd was the "cowboy" there. His ranch was just up above us. So every time he went to town or went back to take care of his cattle, he had to come by the ranch. He stopped by every time.

The way he tells it, the way that we first met was, this other girl and I were sitting out on the fence, at the entrance to the ranch, not knowing there was anybody else in the whole country. And I kept saying I hear music coming down the road, I hear music.

Here come this herd of bulls with Boyd behind them. And here we were sitting on the gate, where he wanted to put his bulls through.

So he said, Pardon me, ma'am, would it be all right if I turn my bulls in here?

And I said, Well, I don't know. I'm not the owner. You'll have to ask him.

Well, what he meant, I learned later, was: Get the hell out of the way! And he got us out of the way. And he got his bulls through the gate. And that's the way that we met.

That summer Boyd provided the horses for a pack trip for the dudes. And we had a good time riding together. So that fall I stayed through the hunting season. And we decided to get married.

Everybody said that it would work about a week. One week would be "pretty good," they said; if it lasted that long it would be a miracle.

A city girl and a cowboy!   .

His family objected more than my family did. They thought it was terrible. But we got married.

Somehow this improbable couple, we just tackled all the ups and downs. That was a million years ago.

Then after World War II we had our war baby. And we set off for Jackson Hole to settle down. Right in the middle of the winter. But we didn't know what to do. We didn't have a job. Or anything else. But in his youth Boyd had worked for the Forest Service rounding up wild horses—as well as with cattle— and so he got a job with the Game Department and we lived in a Ranger cabin one summer. It was beautiful. I would go down to the spring to get the water and every once in a while I'd meet a moose.

But one night Boyd came in and he said, Anne, I'm resigning in the morning. And I gulped a couple of times.

I said, Why?

And he said, I have reported the corruption in the Game Department. They have every racket in the world going on, from selling beaver hides to hay. And he said, I've just had it. I've reported it all the way up to the top and I'm getting out.

And the next day he went in, and he told them. And he resigned.

That's when we decided we'd go to look for a ranch. In Montana. That was in the fall of 1950.

Boyd's idea of ranching was to get a ranch and then build it up, to improve it, to a real ranch. And then move on. So when we first came to Montana we had conflicting ideas. Because I think a woman's idea is always to settle down and Boyd, he always wanted to move on.

Maybe that was the cowboy way. It was in his family.

To look for a ranch we got a real estate guy who was very talkative and he kept talking of this ranch that we wouldn't be interested in because it was forty miles from town. On an unimproved road. No electricity. No conveniences. And nobody in his proper mind would want it. But it sure was a good buy.

Boyd said he'd like to see it and he drove out and when he came back he said, That's the ranch.

So we got it for five dollars an acre. That was cheap even in 1950. And we moved out there with the three small children. And with no electricity and no water in the house.

It was just great!

The first winter we lived on nothing. Oh, we had about five hundred dollars, cash, to get by on through that first winter. And I loved it. I loved building our very own ranch. Of course it was pretty romantic, to start with. The honeymoon and all that. But the reality was better than the romantic dream for me. It was self-fulfilling. We made the dream.

People who have romantic dreams of the West, they come out for a few years, then they go when their dream is met with the hard reality. They become disillusioned. Those people want something that is unreal. No troubles. No problems. No real life situation. They are the ones that go.

To me, the reality of the West surpassed the fantasy dream. Because Boyd and I, we made our own reality.

All my life I wanted to live in the country. There was never any doubt in my mind that was the way I wanted to live. Eventually I knew that living in the West was what I wanted, and Boyd was the one I wanted to live with.

We did it together. We made our dreams, our lives.

One ranch woman remembered how as a girl in St. Louis she had read a pulp magazine, Ranch Romances. *And she dreamed of marrying a cowboy the way that some young girls dreamed of marrying a famous movie actor, or an oil millionaire. To her, it seemed as though there was nothing as romantic as becoming a ranch wife in the legendary land of the cowboys. And so she went west. And she married a cowboy. And she lives, till this day, in a ranch house without electricity.*

And, she says, she loves it.

Jenny Vincent's journey to a ranch in a little mountain village in northern New Mexico was no less romantic. Her odyssey was simply more complex and more unlikely.

She came from a family whose genealogy began in this country with Reverend Roger Williams of Salem, the founder of Rhode Island. Her family's ancestry goes back twelve or thirteen generations to the Puritan fathers and mothers. And her journey to a small dirt ranch, if only a dude ranch, was a long one from her staid and proper origins, come, as she did, on a pilgrimage in search of D. H. Lawrence's ghost.

During the years she has lived in the valley north of Taos, she has become what she searched for. Her quest reminded me of the words of the missionary's wife, Narcissa Prentiss Whitman, who wrote in her Oregon Trail diary of 1836:

"Do not think I regret coming. No, far from it. I would not go back for the world. I am contented and happy, notwithstanding I sometimes get very hungry and weary."

Love of the land is blind, too.

Coming to the Valley
Jenny Vincent

My coming to the valley happened in a strange way. Frieda, D. H. Lawrence's widow, brought me to the valley.

That sounds like a long way round? It was. My former husband and I were on a "Lawrence trek," in 1936; we were following his path around the world. And we had been to Germany and had visited with Frieda's sister. That spring we were in Cornwall, living in the little house on the sea coast where Frieda and Lawrence had lived, and where Katherine Mansfield and John Middleton Murry had lived, when out of the blue we got a letter from Frieda inviting us to New Mexico.

Our plan had been to go to Italy and follow Lawrence's journey to India and Australia. But the Ethiopian war broke out. Things were getting pretty tense in the world. So we decided to go directly to New Mexico and to visit with Frieda.

That was the end of our "Lawrence trek" and the beginning of the new era in our lives. As ranch owners.

North of Taos, in the mountains, there was a little ranch that Mabel Dodge Luhan had given to Frieda and Lawrence. That's where Frieda was living, in the house with the buffalo painted on it, the one Trinidad had painted.

D. H. Lawrence's ashes had been brought back to the ranch that spring. His ashes were to be placed in the chapel that had been built on the ranch. And there was a plot by Lady Brett and Mabel to prevent his ashes from ever getting to the chapel. They thought Lawrence'd turn over if he knew his ashes were being placed in a chapel, by Frieda.

So we visited with Frieda and she invited us to stay with her. And we had a delightful, really delightful, time. We got to know her quite well. She told us a lot of personal things about her relationship with Lawrence, how *Lady Chatterley's Lover* had been very autobiographical. And things like that.

Well, Frieda had a man working for her by the name of Diego Ariano, who lived in a little village in the valley, by the name of San Cristobal. He rode back and forth from the village on horseback every day.

One day, on a horse we had rented from Lady Brett, and another horse, we rode home with Diego. He went down this little road in the valley. And we asked him where that little road went, up above his house.

And he said, "Oh, there's a ranch up there. Nobody has lived in it for a long time. It's abandoned."

The ranch was for sale, as we found out from Ted Mackie, who ran the general store in the valley with his wife, who was the postmistress. And Ted took us in his pickup truck, with us riding in the back of the truck, up the old road to the ranch. It was a very narrow road.

So we rode up to the ranch. There was the beautiful, little two-room house with a porch running across the front, by a mountain brook. It had a couple of outbuildings and a corral. And it was surrounded by fir trees. And that was the beginning of our life in the valley, right there and right then.

One of the things about the ranch that appealed to us was that here was a rugged kind of life. No electricity. No telephones. No running water, except for the mountain brook. No cement pavements. No automobiles in most of the houses in the valley. No radios.

And we loved it.

On the cluttered piano bench, under the current Stock Breeders' Handbook, *was Johann Sebastian Bach's music for the harpsichord. There were piles of music sheets on top of the ancient upright piano, in disorderly stacks, some of them one foot high. And on the tables and on the floor of the living room of the ranch house, and the bedroom, and even in the bathroom, there were piles of books, falling over one another. Some of the books were in bookcases, but the shelves would not hold them all.*

That ranch house of Ellen Cotton's in no ways resembled that of a television program like "Bonanza." After all, the Cartwright ranch on "Bonanza" was a world of men. It was rare for any ranch on television, or in the movies, to have any women, or books, of significance in it. Such things were not masculine.

But the women who came west from the schools and universities of the East brought their own worlds with them. They surrounded themselves with books and music. And the more remote the ranches may have been, the more important their books and music were to them.

Most of these women did not come out west, as the men so often did, to escape from the humane ways of civilization. To rough it. To go back to nature. To hide from themselves. If anything, the women came in the hope that in the freer air and open spaces of the western atmosphere they might be freer, and more open, in exploring their identity as women. And so it might be said that they came west not in search of the West, but in search of themselves.

So it was for Ellen Cotton. That was what she sought. That was what she found in the Montana hills.

And I Hated to Be a Girl
Ellen Cotton

Being a girl, I just hated it when I was a kid. Of course! I just despised it. I wouldn't play with the girls and I played with the boys. And I hated to be a girl. I just hated it! I hated it! Because I could see that all my life I was going to have to wear dresses and do up my hair and all those things. That's the way it was for a girl, in those days. And that's all you had to look to.

Fortunately I came out west when I was just fourteen. And in the West a girl could do almost all the things that a boy could do. On a ranch that was all right. And so that's when I got my first pair of Levi's.

My God!

Mother, she frowned on my wearing Levi's. She was kind of hard-nosed about it. She was against my "wearing your father's pants," she said.

Then more and more people began coming out here, to these dude ranches. Respectable people, from the East, as my mother said. And it got to be acceptable for a woman to be seen wearing a pair of Levi's.

Once I told my mother she ought to have put me out for adoption when I was eight years old, in the ranch country, out here. She was snorty about me saying that.

But I came reconciled to being a female when World War II came. I was appalled by men having to go off to war and kill each other. And doing war things. That's when I thought: That's one advantage to being a female. And that was the first time I consciously could accept to being a female.

A woman!

There were times when I'd thought being a female was a great handicap. But then I decided it doesn't matter who you are. Just be what you are. And be satisfied.

I come from Concord, Massachusetts. That's an old town. Settled in 1630. And people come from everywhere to see where the American Revolution started. On that bridge. They come to see those old buildings. All my life I have seen that. My family had lived there for some time. And my family had been marrying so damn close to their own kind that my first cousin and I, we were both interested in livestock, so we said, It's about time we got some crossbreeding in our family.

So I went out to get some crossbreeding. And how! I did the out-crossbreeding up to the hilt.

Oh, gosh. Oh, gosh. My first husband was a composer. Robert Delaney. He and Stephen Vincent Benét had a Guggenheim fellowship together. They were in Paris at the same time. But they didn't know each other because they were in different fields. Anyway, my husband wrote a choral symphony to Benét's poem on John Brown. It is a honey of a piece. And Bob and Benét got the Pulitzer Prize on that "John Brown." Then Bob did another on "Western Star" and he tried for a Pulitzer on that. But he didn't get it.

Oh, gosh. Oh, gosh. Benét, he was one of the real ones. Those were good years. Oh, gosh.

Now Bob's music is sitting in the warehouse, in Sheridan, Wyoming. There are some ways I think he was the best American composer. But I haven't known what to do with his music. After he and I finally were divorced, he died. So I just stored away his music.

For some time we had been having troubles, because of this rural thing in me. That wouldn't leave me be.

Music is the second biggest thing in my life. And I tried to help him with his music. I really, really tried. But, I thought, I was such a failure. I couldn't play. I couldn't sing. Not as well as I should have to help him.

So I got discouraged.

And when you get discouraged you begin to revert back to your older instincts and I began to revert back to the land. And the critters. That was a thing I thought I had given up. I had had all that when I was a child. Being able to ride and all that and I thought, Hell! I had given that up and I would help him with his music—for the rest of my life. But I couldn't do it.

So I reverted to my first love of livestock and land. My family had had a ranch in Sheridan for years. Since 1893. And I got to come out there once when I was fourteen and I guess I never really got over it.

And so, when Bob and I split up, I came out for one year and had an affair with a rancher I later married. He was contracting for hay. All that summer, I worked for him. I drove a big old Clydesdale mare and a stallion and a sulky rig and a buck rig and I loved it. And I got to stay on. The rancher, he was a lot older than I was, and he wanted me to marry him.

But I just thought, No! I was not going to marry anybody. Then I had three small children and I thought, No, no! this won't do. So I consulted with one cousin of mine and she said, No, don't rush into another marriage. And so I went back east and had some psychiatry.

But I thought finally that the only cure for me was to get back out to this country. To the land. To the critters. And to stay.

So I came out, for good.

The fabled "Lady from Philadelphia" was not a myth. She and her sisters from Boston, Cincinnati, and St. Louis were as real as was the fictional heroine of "The Bride Comes to Yellow Sky," and they often seemed just as happily out of place. One traveler in the West, in the 1880s, observed: "Few women are found on ranches, the necessary isolation and hardships being too masculine for 'feminine tastes.' " Women were "too civilized."

Many of the ladies from the East were simply not prepared by an "artificial and pernicious course of education" for the "life of nature," on a homestead ranch, wrote Eliza Farnham in her Life in the Prairie, *in 1846: "They cannot endure the sudden and complete transition which is forced on them by emigration to the West."*

But, she and they learned.

In The Story of a Pioneer *by Anne Shaw there is a frightening description of how her mother, arriving at the ranch her father had built for them, went into shock and sat for hours with her head in her hand. "She seemed to have died and to have returned to us from the grave," the daughter said.*

And the cowmen and cowhands were not always the most sensitive to these traumas of their women. The coming of a Victorian lady on the stagecoach or the railroad was the occasion for an enthusiastic welcome, for carousing and drunken revelry, a ritual celebration like a Roman holiday in honor of a vestal virgin.

So the day his father brought his mother to their New Mexico ranch is described by William Lumpkin.

When the Old Man Brings
His Bride Out West
William Lumpkin

My mother said to me she came out west on the train to marry my father and landed in Clayton, New Mexico. The cowboys from my father's ranch were there, lined up along the tracks. They had gone two weeks without bathing. Or shaving. Or anything. And they were shooting off their guns and raising the ruckus for the old man when he brings his bride out west.

And she thought these cowboys were the wildest-looking, most uncivilized men she'd ever seen. She was a young lady of Philadelphia.

They had this buggy to take them out to the ranch, which was some twenty miles from Clayton. She said that on the trip the thing that really horrified her was that they got out to Cimmaron, there, and the river was running muddy, brackish, with water from the range, and the cowboys' horses were all drinking it, and the cowboys all jumped off their horses and began to drink that water.

She was eighteen years old.

My Uncle Jim had been the manager of the Matador Cattle Company, which was a Scottish company out of Edinburgh, Scotland. And my father had come out and he worked for the Matador in 1878. And gradually he got his own ranch. And that was when he brought my mother out from Philadelphia.

But all of those Walker girls from Philadelphia came out here, and married early-day ranchers.

In those days the women in our family were independent. They learned to be.

My mother's aunt was awarded a Congressional Medal of Honor for her work in the Civil War. She had been a doctor during the war.

She was the only woman who ever got the Medal of Honor. They had awarded it to her sometime after the Civil War. And then they had taken it away from her because she wasn't a soldier or something like that.

President Carter has just ordered the army to reinstate it. After all these years.

That aunt, she was my mother's father's sister. She was Davy Crockett's cousin. And she lived to be one hundred and seven years old. I saw her just before she died, in 1916.

And my mother came from that tradition.

Of the character of the ranch woman the Honorable John Minto of Oregon spoke a bit ruefully in 1906: "She had another acquirement not usual to womanhood. She could use a rifle, with effect."

In the early years of ranching it was expected that a woman would know how to shoot, to defend herself, or to hunt game.

Men appreciated the woman who was a good shot. They did not consider it to be unladylike; for it might save their lives; it was the sign of a good wife.

The son of an old Colorado rancher told me: "It was the women who defended our homestead with rifles. My grandmother used to tell that the men always were out riding the fences or moving the stones from one place to another. So the women had to defend the ranch.

"No one gave it much of a thought," he said.

It was the men in the East who were fascinated by women with guns in the West. That may be the source of the fame of Annie Oakley and Calamity Jane. For these were women who dressed, behaved, cursed, and shot like men. They were exhibited like freaks in the circus.

Now, why they fascinated some men, I don't know. But they still do, as William Lumpkin so joyously shows in a wonderful story that might have been a myth or legend, if it were not true.

She Shot Him
William Lumpkin

Old man Hurd who owned the ranch on the south face of the Capitan Mountains, he owned all the water there. And one old rancher tried to buy him out, for years he tried to get him out of there. But he never could. So, finally, he hired a couple of killers to come in there, and to kill him. One night they waited for him, when he came home, and they riddled him.

They got the bloodhounds from Santa Fe down and put them where those killers had waited, you know. And they traced them to the old rancher's barn.

Everybody knew he'd hired the killers to kill old Hurd. But the killers had disappeared. They could never even get a bill against the old rancher.

Old Hurd had this daughter, Ann, who was a little older than I was. He had sent her back east, to school. Well, Ann mulled over her father's death and maybe a year later she met the old rancher in town, on the street, in front of the bank. And she pulled out a six-shooter and shot him through the shoulder and he fell down. He was a little bitty, old, short Englishman. Well, Ann, she just stood there and emptied this gun at him.

And she never did hit him.

It was Saturday. So there were a lot of people around. There was half a dozen witnesses that saw it.

So, they arrested her. And she had to go for trial before our old judge where my oldest brother was law clerk.

My brother, he told me this story.

So the old judge called her up to the bench and he said, Now, young lady, he said, according to the law of New Mexico you did attempt to take this man's life with a deadly weapon. And I am going to have to sentence you. And I am going to sentence you to a year and a day. And I am going to commute the sentence.

But, I wish to hell, the old judge said, I could sentence you to six months of target practice.

Her husband died. She could have sold the ranch in New Mexico. She could have moved to town, or gone to California, with what was left after the inheritance tax. And she could have lived fairly easily. But Madlyn Cauhape wanted none of that. In her heart she felt she owed it to her children to keep the ranch going. And besides, she had always been an independent-minded woman and she wasn't about to change now. She loved the ranch.

"Me, live in town? What in the heck would I do in town?" she scoffed.

So she stayed on the ranch, ran it well, earned the respect of her neighboring ranchers and eventually was elected president of their "sheep men's" association in the state. In doing all that Madlyn Cauhape was not unique. By 1978 there were 133,000 women running farms and ranches in the United States. By 1985, it is estimated that one-tenth of all the farms and agricultural businesses in the country will be run by women.

The lonely widow who ran a lonely ranch was no longer alone.

She was part of a new breed of women who were self-reliant and independent.

Nonetheless, she didn't want to be thought of as a "tough and ornery old biddy with a shotgun," the stereotype of women who ranched alone. So she hid her shotgun behind her piano.

"I like ranching," she said. "And I happen to be a woman. That's all."

Being a Woman Rancher Is Interesting
Madlyn Cauhape

My husband died eight years ago today. I was determined not to become dependent. And I have been running the ranch ever since.

For a woman, running a ranch after her husband dies isn't that hard. It's something she has been a part of for most of her life. She is familiar with it. And so it's easier for her, taking over after her husband, than if he was a doctor or lawyer. On a ranch the husband and wife are more likely to be partners.

It is true that in "western" movies the women of the West are either the barroom women, or schoolteachers, or some old, tough biddy who takes a shotgun to you when you walk in the door. For that reason I moved our shotgun away from the front door.

Rarely are women shown as ranchers' wives or ranchers. That's the reason I am interested in this chapter in this book, the "Sisters of Ruth."

Sometimes I will be the only woman at a Wool Growers' meeting. I was the only woman who has been state president of the Wool Growers. And a man will stare at me, at those meetings, with big eyes, as if to say, Now, what's that old biddy doing here? Then, another man, he will look at me and pretend I don't exist. He will just ignore me. Which was hard when there I was chairing the meeting. But some, even if they are simply amazed, will treat me with respect.

Men respect me, I find, if they respect their wives. If a man thinks that his wife is halfway intelligent, then he is likely to think the same of me. But, the man who thinks his wife is a little dumb bunny, he will likely try to treat me the same way.

Being a woman rancher is interesting. Very interesting.

The ranch woman was the forgotten woman of the West. She was largely ignored and overshadowed by her gaudier sisters, the schoolmarm and the whore of western tales. Her unique contribution to ranch life, as a woman, has rarely been recognized and never eulogized. But, as a woman, she was more than the "culture bearer" of books and piano lessons. She did more than share the work of men—which she did. She changed it— as men could not.

Men said, A woman on the place, it changes things. But they did not say how, or why.

Changes that women brought to the West were subtle, but their influence was strong and enduring. It still persists. And it did not consist merely of refinements such as Sunday clothes for church, and the prohibitions of morality or alcohol.

In the way that women looked upon ranching, and practiced it, there was a difference from the ways of men. So, too, there was a difference in the way they believed that life ought to be lived.

On the deserts of the Billy the Kid country, near the Mexican border, where Rita and Janaloo Hill run their ranch, the land is known for its macho. It is a man's country. And yet, these remarkable women were quite aware and articulate in expressing their feeling about the uniqueness of women ranching in such a no man's land.

"Because we are women doesn't make us any better," said Rita Hill. "Maybe, it makes us just a little more human."

Maybe Women Look at It a Little Different
Rita and Janaloo Hill

RITA: Now, on this ranch, we don't have no men. There's just Janaloo and me here.

JANALOO: I work the cattle. That's the job I like.

RITA: Some men, they think we are a little peculiar. That two women, mother and daughter, can't run a ranch.

JANALOO: But we can.

RITA: Maybe women do look at ranching a little bit different. Like all the calves we have has its own name. We know them all by name.

JANALOO: And we always worry about selling the little bitty calves too young. They that buy them don't treat them right and we worry about their being treated right. I don't mind their being eaten because they don't care what happens after they're slaughtered. That doesn't bother me a bit. It's the way they're treated before they're slaughtered. It's the ways they're joused in the sale rings and being hauled on trucks long distances and not allowed to rest and being joused in the packinghouse yards and just generally being mistreated before they ever get in those slaughterhouses. That does worry us.

RITA: Some of the calves we have, these yearlings, there's one little bitty spot-faced one; he's real cute. I said to Janaloo, Maybe we ought to butcher him by ourselves, so he isn't mistreated by someone, someplace. He's such a good-tempered little fellow.

Anyhow, we are a little bit peculiar you know. Being women.

JANALOO: I believe some men ranchers do feel this way, deep down, this same way we do. But they'd be ashamed to say they feel this way.

RITA: One fellow I know, he knows all his animals by name. A good rancher, he's got to know all the peculiarities of his animals. So a lot of ranchers, they do know their animals that way.

JANALOO: And I know quite a few ranchers, you can tell they feel for their animals. But they are a little bit ashamed to say it. While others don't feel it. They are a little bit callous about what happens to their animals.

RITA: A man may feel that shows a soft streak, I suppose. But it really doesn't.

JANALOO: Ranchers, they need a woman, sometimes, to show them human ways.

RITA: Some women with independent ways of thinking probably contributed a good bit to ranching. Because they contributed another viewpoint to the one that their husbands had. And that helps.

No man can know too much. There is always something that one person knows another doesn't. There are some people who have what you call education—whatever that is—who feel they know more than anyone else. Men sometimes feel that way. But the experience of people, of men and women, are all different. So everyone knows some things that others do not.

And women, you know, they know some things, too.

School Days

7

School Days
Ellen Cotton

Schoolhouses were the center of our social activity in this here particular part of the country. They would have dances and 4-H Club meetings and parties and the kids would put on shows. Everybody would gather around. In the old days when you had to go there by horse and wagon, it was quite a few miles, through bad weather, well, entertainment was a luxury.

Oftentimes you went to quite a lot of effort for it. Because you entertained yourself.

And the kids would come along too. They would sleep over sometimes, in the schoolhouse.

When we lived up at Beaver Creek there was an awful nice school there. I think we had about ten kids in the school. Not many more. And the teacher was a rancher's wife and she lived across of the road from the schoolhouse. She just loved to teach. She loved that school. She loved those kids.

Gosh! She spent about half of her salary on those kids. Every time that we had a party that teacher would bring in beautiful cakes and presents for those kids. And at Christmastime, oh, my gosh! what she did for those kids.

That's why, I think, she was such a good teacher. She was not an intellectual person at all, but she loved the kids. You would go to school and you wouldn't think much was going on, but when the kids got through her school they would go on to high school and get good marks and a lot of those kids went right on to college.

There wasn't any of the ghastly pressure that you have now. And things they had to learn just sort of soaked into them along the way somehow.

Being a little school it wasn't the big kids against the little kids. Even to play any kinds of games at recess the big kids had to let the little kids participate. Otherwise there won't be enough kids to play. And so the big kids would help the little kids and show them how to do things. In the school the big kids would often help the little kids with their work, and stuff. That was good too, because they got to working together. Instead of everyone being against each other.

My kids all went to that school. It seemed to me everything in our country school worked out so well.

And I remember when she taught the kids math, she related it to the grain and cattle and ranch life the kids were used to dealing with. That way it all made sense to them.

It seems to me that there are always a few kids who can get high grades and can memorize things and be good students. But a lot of kids have difficulty memorizing things. They get things in a different way. Seems like we ought to have other ways of getting knowledge for those kids who can't get it quickly. In the old country schools it was like that.

Learning isn't a matter of getting A's. It is translating the things which you learn into real life. And teaching is something that should help you in living. That's what it is all about.

And that's why the old schoolhouse was more than a place for "education." It was a place for the whole community.

Since the coming of television all of that has changed. They don't have any of those old neighborhood activities in schoolhouses that were there. They don't have the gatherings that we used to. They don't have any dances anymore.

All that is gone. It's just too bad. Of course, when television came it was such a big thing. Everybody couldn't bear not to watch it. You just stayed home and you watched television. And it became a kind of habit. Nobody hardly visited anymore. And if you did have a dance hardly anybody would come.

And the schoolhouse was closed up. It is empty now.

On the hills the one-room schoolhouse stood alone. It looked like a Puritan church.

The old frame building, with its frugal design and its clean, white painted clapboards, had an innocence that was at once peaceful and righteous. If it had a steeple it might easily have been mistaken for a place of worship. But that would not have been a mistake. The one-room school in many ways was like a church, a meeting place where a spirit of neighborliness and morality were taught.

The rural school, on Beaver Creek, that Ellen Cotton remembered, was typical of so many. In the rough hills of the cattle rangeland on the Wyoming border, that little school was surely the heart and soul of its community. It had to be. There was no other.

Romantic as Ellen Cotton's memory may be, it was not wholly nostalgic. Nor was it necessarily untrue.

One time in my youth I attended not a one-room, but a four-room, country school. In some ways it was like going to church. And I still remember, with a warm feeling, the sense of neighborliness and respectability it inspired in me.

Not everyone has as fond memories of the one-room school. To some it seemed a backward and narrow-minded place. And they looked back begrudgingly. Old-time rancher Spike Van Cleve, of Big Timber, Montana, offered this caustic comment on his memory of such a school.

"Hell. I went to a one-room, eight-grade, country school, and I damn sure don't think the older kids taught the younger. Certainly not with intent; it was just that little kids listened. . . ."

One of the most down-to-earth descriptions of the old one-room school was found in a report of the state of North Dakota, in 1890. Of the nearly 1,500 schools, two were still sod houses, made of dirt, forty were simply log cabins, thirty were not schools at all, but met in local ranch houses, seventeen were city schools of brick, and the rest were plain frame buildings.

In the classrooms more than three hundred of these schools had no dictionaries. Sixteen had no blackboards. And only forty-three of the schools had libraries. That was less than five percent.

Since attendance at school wasn't compulsory, half of the children didn't go. Of those who did, half of them never got past the first grade.

Then, why on earth were these one-room schools so fondly remembered by so many of their pupils? It may have been because the parents and pupils and teachers built the schools by themselves. And so, the schools, for better or worse, belonged to them.

Remembering their schooldays, both Robert Skinner, Sr., and Jr., proudly boasted that one of the earliest schools in their ranching community in eastern Oregon was on their ranch. The school was their ranch house. And they were both its teachers and pupils.

In the beginning these schools of the homesteaders were always their homes. The educational system was the earth itself, and the natural world. And they well might have exclaimed, as did the good duke in Shakespeare's As You Like It:

> *Finds tongues in trees, books in the running brooks,*
> *Sermons in stones . . .*

The Skinner family on their ranching homestead would have understood that sort of educational system.

Schoolroom in the Ranch House
Robert Skinner, Sr., and Robert Skinner, Jr.

GRANDFATHER: In the early years when my brothers and sisters were going to school my dad, he just hired a teacher to come to the ranch. And that's how my mother got here. She came from Scotland. She came to teach. She taught first at the Ruby Ranch. Then after she and Dad were married they had a schoolroom up in the old ranch, here. On the third floor. A special room in the ranch, for a school.

And a lot of these neighbors' kids, they came too. They'd ride horses over to the ranch house. They'd get here whenever they could.

Then, later, they built the one-room schoolhouse. And everybody went to it, as best they could, by horse and wagon.

FATHER: One of the things we take for granted today is the school bus. We forget what it was like going to school on cold mornings, by horse and wagon, in an open buckboard.

When I was young it was seven, or eight, miles over a rough road to the one-room schoolhouse. Sometimes when we couldn't go by car, Dad would send us with someone in a buggy or horse and wagon. Sometimes we couldn't go at all if the road was bad, or snowed in.

GRANDFATHER: In the morning you'd wake up to the sound of those iron tires of the wagons on the snow. You could hear them screaming for a mile. When it was cold they had a distinct scream to them. And that is one sound I will never forget: the old iron wagon wheels screaming on the cold snow.

FATHER: And going to bed, in that cold bed, and getting up on that ice-cold floor, to go to school.

GRANDFATHER: Going to school wasn't easy then, as it is now.

FATHER: Memories that we have of our childhood, and our rural background, when we look back we say, That was all great. But the tendency has been to get away from all that. In school, you know, they taught us that there was an easier life in the city. They always said, Get an education so you won't have to work for a living. It was a terrible thing to tell children. Because they sort of used our own schools against us.

Besides, it's not true. There's no such thing. There isn't anything that's going to replace work as far as I'm concerned. Maybe you won't be working on the end of a pitchfork. But, you'll still have to work.

The rural people, they looked forward to that something "better" that they were taught about. And they thought, well, if the city life did that, well, it tended to draw a lot of them away from ranching. So they moved to the city.

And we learned that in school. To look for that "better" life.

GRANDFATHER: There aren't many of the country schools left now. I guess you could say they put themselves out of business.

On those high plains of the Texas panhandle where he grew up, the son of a homesteading rancher who became the editor of Harper's *magazine, remembered how the first schoolhouse was built in his rural community. "The neighborhood plainly needed a school, so the men built one," John Fischer said.*

And it was as easy as that. If a school was needed, then you built it. No one else would.

Nor was a schoolhouse thought to be the responsibility of the whole community. Those who had the children did the building: you would not expect a man who raised sheep to pay for the barn of some man who raised cattle.

As the old saying went: Let them as has children educate them.

That may be why the country schoolhouses were scattered far and wide across the countryside. Schools came to the pupils, not pupils to the schools.

Now as we look back it seems hard to believe that there were no federal, state, and county officials and regulations that told the people what to do—and how. They just did it.

And that was not so long ago.

In her tales of how her neighbors built the schoolhouse in her ranch village after World War II, Jenny Vincent remembered that even then rural people wanted such schools. But building a school was more than a mastery of carpentry. The people sometimes had to construct a curriculum as well, supply the books if necessary, and if there were not enough teachers, do that too.

And that's what they did.

Building a School
Jenny Vincent

When we first came to the valley there was a one-room school. Then they built a newer school that had two rooms. But they only had one teacher. That was in '41. So we had a meeting of the people in the valley to talk about whether or not we all thought that it would be nice to have a bigger school, a "real" school.

And the people decided that a larger school would be great. Because they didn't like their kids having to go into Taos, fifteen miles away.

In the winter it was a difficult trip. The roads were bad. And we didn't have the transportation into town which we have today.

So we decided to build a school.

All the men in the valley worked on the school building. So did the children. The stones came from the fields. The tiles came from the state penitentiary. And either by laying stones and tiles, or by plastering, or doing woodwork, by building desks, everybody helped.

We got textbooks from the public schools. The county schools were very interested and they welcomed our school. They got us the hot lunch program, which was just new that year.

But they had just this one teacher in the valley. And she could only handle four grades. So they asked us if we would teach grades fifth through eighth. Even though we had only planned to try to teach high school, we did it.

And all the kids in the valley, they came to that school. They had no bus transportation. They walked up, all the way up the valley, and walked home again after school.

I was teaching in the elementary school. Believe it or not, I was teaching Spanish to the Spanish-speaking kids. I didn't know Spanish. I was learning it from the books while I was teaching it. Even though teaching Spanish was not really allowed in the public schools, at that time. But none of us were really teachers.

We had that school going for, oh, three years. It was really our school. From the ground up.

Can you imagine a schoolboard letting rural people, these days, build their own school? And teach in it? By themselves?

The prim schoolmarm, a proper young miss, as chaste and virginal as the white lace collar on her modest black dress— it is a familiar memory. But, what that pristine picture did not take into account was that the schoolmarm was often a lonely and vital woman, as down-to-earth as the ranching communities in which she taught. And she was often the only single woman.

In 1875 the Santa Fe New Mexican *published an item that offered a different portrait of the schoolmarm:*

"Now then, children," said a parish schoolmistress, showing her children off on examination day, "who loves all men?" "You, missus," came the unexpected reply.

And the frontier newspaper editorialized: "New Mexico is not the only place where the schoolmaster is abroad."

Some of that lusty and exuberant spirit of the young men and young women who went courting in the homestead years was captured by Omar Barker in his reminiscence of schoolmarms and their cowboy lovers in the New Mexico ranch country that he grew up in.

Maybe things were less puritanical in New Mexico than elsewhere, but there is no evidence of that.

Every Cowpoke Wanted a Schoolmarm
Omar S. Barker

Nowadays many of the old one-room *escuelas* (schools) are being abandoned for modern consolidated schools to which some children are daily hauled twenty miles or more and back in buses. Doubtless there will always be fine Christmas programs in the bigger, new schools, too, but never can whole groups of teachers be quite the Christmas inspiration that single lone schoolmarms of the one-room schools were 'most all over the cow-country West.

I say "single schoolmarms" advisedly, because in the old bronc and buckboard days many a cowboy wintered on a ranch instead of drifting south with the sunshine solely because of the smiles of some single newcomer schoolmarm.

"Whenever I was on the schoolboard in them days," an old-timer once told me, "I always favored hirin' the best lookin' young unmarried schoolmarms from the East that we could get. I always figgered that the more we could fix it for cowboys to marry gals with enough sense and education to teach school, the better it was for the country.

"Not only that, but I owned a half-interest in an outfit that sold buggies and buckboards, and every time we fetched in a new schoolmarm, two or three lovesick cowboys was purt' near sure to buy them a new rig to take her ridin' in!

"Speakin' of schoolmarms and Christmas," continued the old-timer, "did I ever tell you about me and Lucy? She was a schoolmarm. Come all the way out from Indiany. Purtiest head of dark red hair you ever seen on a heifer! 'Course, I started courtin' her right from the start. But so did some other cowpokes better lookin' and not as bashful as I was.

"Along in December the schoolmarm announced she was fixin' to have the scholars put on a program at the schoolhouse Christmas Eve, and everybody was invited. It also became known that she was havin' all the kids write letters to Santa Claus telling him what they wanted most for Christmas. She told them if they would be reasonable and not ask for too much she would sure do her best to get Santa Claus to come through with it.

"That gave me an idea. I set down and wrote a little letter to ol' Santy my ownself. I slipped it under the schoolhouse door one evening after the teacher left.

"Well, she set the program for early in the evening so the littler kids could stay 'wake and so there'd be plenty of time left for the dance that some of us cowpokes had cooked up for afterward. I don't recollect how come I did get there a little late—honin' the nicks out of my ol' Wade & Butcher razor, maybe—but when I come in a little yaller-haired gal scholar was up there on the platform readin' those letters to Santy Claus, and when she comes to mine she read it just like I wrote it, without ever battin' an eye.

" 'Dear Santa Claus: All I want for Christmas is a purty little red-haired schoolmarm.' And of course I'd been fool enough to sign my name to it, and when the little gal read it right out before God and everybody, it like to busted up the meetin'. I never seen any gal blush as hard—nor as purty—as that schoolmarm did. I hadn't aimed to throw my loop quite so public, but as long as I had, I figgered I'd just as well foller it up.

"So the first time I got a chance to dance with her after the kids' program was over, I come right out and laid it on the taw line how I felt about her. That turned out to be her last term of schoolteachin'. We was married right after school let out in the spring—with ol' Tom Ellers, where she boarded, dressed up like Santa Claus to give the bride away!"

Of course not every cowpoke who wanted a schoolmarm for Christmas was that lucky, but whether they were or not a lot of old-timers will tell you that nobody ever did more to make Christmas merry in the cow country than those hard-working schoolmarms. Their Christmas kid programs could bring all kinds of folks together, regardless of feuds and disagreements, in the spirit of Christmas neighborliness and goodwill out here in an essentially lonely land where the cattle were many and the people few.

On the upright piano there was an old family Bible. It was too old now to be opened often. Besides that Good Book there was a volume of Shakespeare's plays and one of Ralph Waldo Emerson's essays. These books had come across the country in the covered wagon pulled by the oxen that great-grandmother had sternly guided to the family homestead. And they too were thought of as practical guidebooks to day-to-day life on the frontier. They were more than books.

In the days when men were mostly unschooled and illiterate they looked on books with awe. They may have respected them all the more because they could not read them.

But the books on most homesteads were few. Even if they had been available most ranchers would not have had much use for them.

Most learning came from doing and listening. These homesteading ranchers made-do in matters of education, by educating themselves and one another, much as they did in everything else. Education was not something they could learn in schools. And even if they could, they would not have trusted it.

Should it have been so surprising that many ranchers married schoolteachers, as Frank Shiveley had done? The marriage of a practical man and an intellectual woman was often a naturally complementary one.

And Marian and Frank Shiveley fondly and vividly remembered how they combined their different ways of learning for their mutual education and entertainment. On their isolated Nevada ranch they had no one to learn from but themselves. And so, as in day-to-day practical things, they learned to make-do in that too.

Marian said it best: "We made our own happiness."

Reading to the Men
Marian and Frank Shiveley

MARIAN: Now what did people do before they had TV's and radios? Well, I will tell you.

In the old days we lived eighty-five miles from the railroad. For six months of the time we were busy getting ready for winter and for the six months of the winter we didn't go anywhere. We just stayed at home. But it didn't bother us. We didn't mind it. We entertained ourselves.

FRANK: One thing is we always had provision in for the winter. So we didn't have to worry about that. We had a year's supply of groceries in the cellar, dug back in the hill.

MARIAN: In the evenings in the winter we were not much for cards. We never did play cards. And, to me, it always seemed a waste of time.

FRANK: We didn't have any money to gamble with. Anyhow.

MARIAN: So what we did was to read books. Aloud. To the men.

I had a cousin who worked in the library in Elko. For twenty-five cents we'd get a library card. Every once in a while I would send in our library fee. And she would mail out four books at a time to the ranch. We would tell her just about what we wanted to read.

After supper, when my sister and I, we had the work done up, we would read the library books aloud. If she did the reading, then I would embroider scarves. The boys would be working on things. She just sat there and read out loud. Then, if she finished that book, it was my turn to read. And I would take the next book, and she'd embroider. That's the way we did it.

The men would braid ropes and tie knots and make bridle reins. And that was the way a lot of our evenings were spent with the women reading and the men listening.

FRANK: We couldn't read anyway.

MARIAN: We read books that everybody'd like. Not especially Wild West. Just a good book. Let's see. We had the *Call of the Wild*. And we had Zane Grey's books. That pleased the boys. And we read animal stories. I remember one about a beaver. We enjoyed that one.

Now, we didn't go in for those love stories. The foolish kind. That would've probably bored the boys.

And that's the way we spent a lot of our evenings in the winter on the ranch. Reading books.

In the wintertime we'd have supper by six o'clock. Then we had three hours after the work was done up to do whatever we wanted before we went to bed at around nine o'clock. So we didn't stay up and we got up really early.

There was one winter when the winter came in the middle of November and we were snowed in till the twelfth of May. I remember that my sister and I went out on the first trip out of the house on Mother's Day. And then it was a question of whether or not we would get over the summit, or not. That's the kind of winters that we had.

Oh, they talk about cabin fever in those days. But we women

went out a lot. We'd don clothes so we could go out with the boys.

FRANK: And we would come by the ranch house and pick 'em up and we'd go out and pitch a little hay.

MARIAN: In those days you had to make your own happiness. That was all there was to it. If we sat there, snowed in, and moped and whined, I don't know what we would've done.

So, we made our own happiness.

Telling a story was a way of learning and teaching, of looking at the world and understanding it, of thinking a thing over until all its fine points and subtleties were known. It was a way of handing down to the next generation the history of the past generation. But, most of all, telling a story was a way for the teller and the listener to get together, to share an experience, and to get to know one another.

Storytelling was more than an entertainment. It strengthened and reaffirmed a sense of community.

Once the mechanical storytellers, the radios and televisions, came into the rural areas, the old storytellers didn't have a chance. The new machines required none of the subtle skill and human understanding that was demanded of the older storyteller and listener. Any child could push a button or turn a knob. The listener no longer felt obligated to listen intently, with respect, to the remote voices of the talking machines.

And the arts of storytelling and listening were doomed. Well, almost. The story of the death of the storytellers among the Spanish ranchers in her mountain valley, which Jenny Vincent told me, is surely a paradox.

She told the story so well.

The End of the Storytellers
Jenny Vincent

Of an evening in the old days the people used to get together on Nick Martinez's porch. They would entertain each other. They would tell stories. And they might begin a story on Monday night and on Tuesday night they would continue it. And they might finish that story in one week. Or in two weeks.

They needed each other. Because if someone talked they needed someone to listen.

In rural society people don't need each other for entertainment anymore. Now they have television.

When we first came into the valley, getting around was a problem. Because people didn't have cars. So they walked to the school, for meetings, or to visit a neighbor. They would go out for a walk of an evening. And they would end up in visiting and talking.

But when television came in no one went out anymore. And there was less and less visiting.

And it got to be so that you could not even have a PTA meeting on a certain night. Because that was fight night. None of the fathers would come.

And with near everybody listening to the same story on television, that was the end of the storytellers.

The schoolhouse was abandoned. Its front door was nailed closed and the nails were rusted. One of its windows was broken, probably by the winter winds. Where children once played, tall grasses grew. Still, it stood as it always had, on the hill, seemingly untouched by time, or by vandals. And if one listened closely one could hear the ghosts of recited lessons echoing high in the beams, and the voices of the children, playing at recess, could be heard in the tall grasses.

Across the country there are thousands of such abandoned schools. Late as 1910 there were said to be 200,000 of the one-room schools still in use in this country. By the end of World War I they began to close in epidemic numbers. By the end of

World War II less than one-tenth of them were left. The passing of the one-room country school, I think, had little to do with educational principles, or needs. It began with the coming of paved roads and motorcars. And it may be fitting that the symbol of this educational change was the new yellow school bus.

"God, how we hated that yellow school bus," said Anne Charter. On her Bull Mountains ranch the busing of rural children to a consolidated school in town meant a trip of thirty miles. Each way. Each day.

"We thought we'd never see our kids again," she said.

When They Closed Our Country School
Anne Charter

I remember when they closed up our country school. One of those little country schools. Everyone was against it here. They sent those school buses to take our kids to the consolidated school, in town. And the kids, they didn't want to go. And we didn't want them to go.

But there was nothing we could do. They didn't ask us. They sure didn't ask the kids either.

The school bus would come and take our kids away and we would sit out here and worry if they ever got there. In the winter when the snows come, there are big drifts everywhere. Sometimes a car gets snowed under.

And a lot of ranchers didn't have telephones. So we never knew if our kids made it to school or not.

We hated that school bus!

And that old country school, well, it had been a part of our community. So when they closed it up, they closed part of our community up. They just ended it. They took something away from our rural way of life. They killed it.

And we never have got it back. It is gone forever.

In the Montana territory, the town of Bannack hung twenty-three men who were accused of 102 murders, in 1864.

That same year the townspeople built their first one-room school-house. On the homesteading frontiers schooling was not thought of merely as education; it was a matter of morality. There were more than the three R's taught in schools. There were four R's —reading, 'riting, 'rithmetic, and righteousness.

Not merely were biblical passages favored texts. The Bible itself was a favored textbook.

Education was more than learning; it was the road to success, it taught the Golden Rule, it encouraged an upright and moral character, it inspired the lazy to become industrious, and it made it possible for a barefooted farmboy to become the President of the United States—as Abe Lincoln had.

One hundred years later more and more ranchers looked with suspicion upon the consolidated schools. As the crusty old Oregon rancher, Glen Sitz, angrily expressed it: They felt these schools were not fair to them. They were troubled by what they thought was their contemptuous view of old-fashioned ranching morality. They believe these schools had betrayed their faith in education.

Something had gone wrong.

Why Do Teachers Teach Them That?
Glen Sitz

Schools is changed now.

One reason the old ways are dying, I think, is the schools. These kids in the schools are brainwashed to a different way of life. I believe that because I've talked to some of the teachers here in town, and they take kids out to the bird refuge, and I read in the newspaper, too, where'd they teach the kids that the former way of life that made this part of the country was wrong. That ranching was wrong. That ranching ruined the West.

Now, I don't think the ranchers destroyed this part of the country. Why do the teachers teach them that?

And I don't think that's true at all. If it hadn't been for our ancestors going west, none of us would be here. Maybe it would still be a wilderness. Maybe that's what they want. But those teachers in those schools, they don't know a thing about ranching.

So they blame us for the destruction of the West. Of the game and fish. Of the land. Of every damn thing.

Well, half of the wild game in the West is raised on our ranches. They don't raise no wild game in those city schools, that I heard of. And as for the fish, the reason there is less fish is there is so many people from the cities come out here to go fishing. And they build all of those dams for electricity for the cities. And nature can't take care of that like it used to do, when it was left alone.

Now, don't get me wrong. I am for education. I believe in that real strong. The rancher, well, education is the only chance we have. Because votewise we don't amount to nothing.

So all we have on our side is to teach the truth about things. And those schools ought to teach the truth.

The Children of Eden

8

Go to the City? I Been
Marion Cauhape

Can I ask you a question: Are you going to stay on the ranch?

Yep.

Why do you want to stay here?

Well, I don't know. I can't imagine me doing anything else.

Ever try?

Not really. I worked down at the Artesia airport. But just for a little bit. And didn't really like it.

Most young people leave the ranch sometimes. Ever want to leave? And go to the city?

I been.

And you never felt like you were in a kind of prison?

Here?

Right. Haven't you ever felt you were hemmed in? And wanted to bust out? And go places?

Well, not really.

And you never wanted to bust out of here?

Never had the inclination to.

As a young man, don't you ever feel isolated out here? That you are missing out on something? Don't you feel confined to the ranch?

No.

Why not?

I feel I would be more confined in doing some job in town.

And there is nothing in town that is all that interesting to me. Being here is a lot more interesting than working on some assembly line. And slapping hubcaps on a car, or doing something like that.

So you stay because you like it? It's not because it's a duty you feel you owe your folks?

When I was a little kid my dad, he used to tell me the day would come when I was going to run this place. And he was going to go fishing. And that's about the only thing I ever thought about.

The quiet young man with the easy smile was one of those no one seemed to be interested in. He was just a ranch boy. He went to the ag school of his state university. He simply wanted to be a rancher. Nothing more. He had not given up a promising career on Wall Street to come west and raise coyotes for fun and profit. He was born on his family's ranch, he grew up there, and he wanted to stay there.

And he said so, in a very few, but choice, words.

And in his own way he was trying to do a heroic thing. There was no harder work on a ranch than keeping it going as one's grandparents and parents had done.

Somehow this young man who stayed and worked on a ranch was not believed to be romantic. He was not a Midnight Cowboy. He was not a Rhinestone Cowboy. He was not a Rodeo Cowboy. And he was not even an Urban Cowboy, the musical movie that John Travolta was to star in.

But, to Marion Cauhape, "that stuff wasn't real." That was all "movie stuff." It "don't grow no meat on sheep and cows" on his family's ranch in the dry range of southern New Mexico.

The real ranching youths, like him, were, however, few at best. And it did look as though they would soon be outnumbered by the Urban Cowboys who had grown up on that "movie stuff." In cattle country there were growing colonies of more and more newcomers, the young people from the countercultures of the cities, who had something the real ranch youth could not have— money.

Some of these newcomers were the children of ranchers. They had left the ranches in the sixties to go to the cities and the universities. And there they had become all sorts of sophisticated and faddist things. The dumb farmboys could be just as dumb as any graduate students from the cities.

It is strange, and yet it is appropriate that these seemingly contradictory young people should be one and the same. They did not really know what was happening to them.

The sensitive and yet somehow angrily sad look of the sons and daughters of the homesteading pioneers was beautifully expressed by Stan Jonasson, from his origins in the Mormon settlements of his family in southern Idaho and northern Utah, the Lands of Deseret.

Of Stan Jonasson's description of the odyssey of his childhood friends and of himself, back and forth between all of these urban and rural worlds, nothing need be said that he does not say. He says it simply, in urban ways.

In some ways young Marion Cauhape and Stan Jonasson are the same young men wearing different masks.

Back to the Land
Stan Jonasson

All of these young people coming in here to go back-to-the-land, the first thing they do is go down to the welfare office and get food stamps. Then it is back-to-the-land. Some of them really do work on the land they want to go back to. That's a whole different group than those that want the welfare state to help them get back-to-the-land. Some of them are my friends.

I feel a closeness to these people. They are my generation.

Now everyone is looking for an identity. And if the identities offered by the urban life-style aren't giving people the energy, the juice, they need, then they may look elsewhere. And so these New York City cowboys become a reality out here. It seems to me that the fabric of American life, in the cities, is disintegrating. But, I wonder if these people are really looking for values from the past, for rural ways of life, or whether they are looking for some kind of fantasies that will hide them from the realities of urban life that is falling apart.

It was different when I was young. It was the opposite.

Sure, when I was younger I had one desire. To get out of here! And I went to Salt Lake City to school. To the Big City! And I never thought I would come back to here. I didn't want to. Never! Never!

Now you get into these young kids and everyone is listening to country music. And everyone is scrounging around for old Hank Williams albums. And they're all wearing cowboy boots, all the way to Hollywood. And they're wearing western hats and western-style clothing.

In the West, when I was a kid, we all thought that was for country hicks. That was dumb.

Suddenly there is this whole kind of thing happening here. Everywhere. And that gives a kind of reinforcement to the life-style that's out here. It's a whole different phenomenon. Certainly it's not universal, but it's affecting a big part of the urban population.

And the people are trying to reinforce traditions and values they never even had before. That makes it hard for some people who come here. Because they have to direct their new life themselves; they have to take the responsibility for it. And they don't know how to. Even a simple thing like a camping trip in the mountains, well, out here, you can't pay someone to set up your tent.

They knocked the shit out of our towns to attract these dudes. All of the dudes who want to go back-to-the-land. But, they don't have to do that, because these people are coming in anyway. They can't control it anymore. They cannot stop it. They are going to destroy the West, like they did where I grew up, because they don't know what the West is all about.

And we're going to help them destroy the West. Because it's money.

People are coming in here for a certain life-style. But if you ride on this growth wave, and a lot of us have ridden it right to the bank, you'll find that the same people who come here for freedom from the cities have taken our freedom away. Because the more people you have in ranch country, the less ranches you have.

Ranching life-style? To me there are some terms that epitomize it. Like "to lay back." It is certainly a slower life-style. One that we like to think of has a little more time for people as individuals. It's a more human kind of life-style.

To me, and to people who have expressed this idea to me, generally those people who live this life-style, out here, they are not ambitious in the middle-class American sense. When you move into a rural area you don't move there to become a concert pianist. If you're going to do anything like that you move to New York and Los Angeles. If you move to Idaho you resolve yourself to the fact you aren't going to be anything spectacular in the eyes of the rest of America. And that's exactly why you do it.

In the *American Horsemen,* I read about this Bell Ranch, in New Mexico, where this fellow said he would like to have a time machine and go back one hundred or more years. And then blow up that time machine! That's a very romantic idea. I think a lot of us would like to do that. But, I won't want to return to a consciousness of one hundred years ago that isn't my own consciousness.

That doesn't mean what they're doing isn't real. By creating a reality of the past that is false, in doing so it may become more real than reality.

I think about that. About the way we look at ourselves, in the West.

When I grew up in this town there was just Mom and Pop neighborhood stores around here. Then in the 1960s, the Circle K's and 7-Elevens and those kinds of convenience stores came in. They ran the family groceries out of business within two, three years.

Suddenly, every city in the West is starting to look the same. Every city has its strip development on the new highway. Every K-Mart looks the same. They all have the same-sized parking lots. And the same buildings that sit in all the same parking lots. Now, what is left of the spirit of western individualism in those parking lots? So it is just like they planned these shopping centers with cookie cutters and they stamped us out to the same mold.

And you look around and what you see is that your life-style is disappearing. So you start grabbing ahold of the things that are important.

In this town when I grew up it was like a big farm town. In a way. But that is not why I identify with the rural way of life. No, it is more a family sort of thing. What is called roots. It is part of the ethic or mystique of life in this part of the country.

May I try to tell you why I think these roots are more important to me now than they were ten years ago? I think it has to do with the fact that our way of life is changing here and all of a sudden instead of people leaving the vanishing West, it is becoming a place where the people are coming to.

And it has become an absolution for urban sins. Nirvana of America.

The sense of the West is locked in the liquid, fluid spine of the earth. It's a sensitivity to the nature of the earth. Of America.

Not one of ten young men or women born on a farm or ranch can hope to earn enough money on their family's place to live on the land they were born on. They have to leave. And that sad statistic of the U.S. Department of Labor, made in the early 1960s, is even sadder today. Those "farm youths who could anticipate such a career [in agriculture] will continue to decline," the government prophets said at the time. And they were right.

One in ten did not offer too much hope for the other nine. And there is even less hope for them today.

Even if they could stay, would ranch youth really want to? After all, the migration to the cities began decades before ranching was reduced to its present status of second-class citizenship.

Most sons and daughters of ranchers would return if they could, insisted Billy Stephenson. They left because they were forced to, he said. And, "given half a chance" to earn a living from the earth, they would come back to their real love, he wistfully added, "I think."

On the sprawling Stephenson I-X Ranch, in the deserts of

New Mexico, where he runs the place with a solitary hired hand, one can almost hear the silence as Billy Stephenson waits, as do so many ranchers, for the return of the prodigal sons and daughters.

Most of Them Would Give Anything to Be Back on the Ranch
Billy Stephenson

On a ranch when you're a teenager maybe you are out there working and you see your friends running around town. So, it might look to you like you're getting the raw end of the deal. And so you might want to run around too. Later on, if you really got ranching in you, you come back to it and you realize that you're a lot happier back on the ranch doing what you want to do and you realize that is what you want to do.

A young kid, he isn't sure what he really wants to do. So they go try different things.

Yah. I can tell you about a dozen kids right around here that the same sort of thing has happened to. When they got out of college, or even if they didn't go to college, they went out to work for maybe a few years. And then later on they'd come back to the ranches.

And most of them say they don't ever want to go back there in the city and do what they were doing. Most just want to stay right here on their ranches. Even though they're not really making money in ranching.

Yah. I think most kids want to stay on the ranches. But they can't.

Most ranches aren't big enough to support more than one family. So the rest of the children, they have to leave. They can't make a living, here.

And I think there's a lot more people who had to leave the ranches that want to come back. But they can't. Most of them would give anything to be back on the ranch, they'd give anything.

As rural sociologist Walter G. McKain has written: "People move beyond the city limits to escape the insecurities of city life, to recapture a romantic ideal, to cut the cost of living, or to get a better place for their children. So they say. In their mind's eye they see an idyllic small community." But, the truth is that they are still "dominated by the central city" and they bring a "metropolitan complex" with them.

"The rural ideal," wrote McKain, "is elusive."

Still, the urban people seeking after "the rural ideal" come in increasing numbers. The less chance they had of ever finding their romantic dream, the more they seemed to search for it.

For a hard-eyed and gruff old-timer, Rex Bundy looked with unusual poignancy on these urban refugees. He did not much like them. He did not want to watch them "cluttering up" his beloved Bitterroot Valley, in Montana. He did not think they'd ever make it back to nature. But he had a begrudging sadness for them.

And it seemed to him that their urban ways simply would not work in the rural countryside. Especially those of the young people. In the city, consumerism was a way of life; when you needed something you just bought it, you didn't make it, or make-do with what you had.

Most of all, Bundy thought, they had lost their closeness to the earth. And so they had lost faith with the power of renewal of nature.

Even at his age, retired from ranch life and rodeoing, he worked as hard as a young man in his garden. He grew beans and potatoes enough for all year. And he did it not just for economic reasons.

"Work's good for you," he said. "If a man stops working he's good as dead."

The Trouble with These Young People
Rex Bundy

Nowadays, the trouble with most of these young people is they don't know how to work. They can't get any satisfaction out of working up a sweat. Or getting their hands dirty. And Christ only knows they don't want to get a backache. I think it is the way they are brought up. I actually do. They've never had to get out, and work. They don't know how.

So, these young people, they've forgotten how to use their hands.

That's what made the human race. That thing there. Your hand. And they've forgotten how to use it. Whether it is the educational system, or whether it is that attitude they have that the world, it's going to all blow up in their faces, so why make the effort to work, I don't know. There are a lot of people, young people, that feel that way. They talk like that and if they talk it, they must have some feeling for it.

As a kid, I come out of high school at the very heart of the Depression. You couldn't beg, borrow, or steal a job. That's what worries me now. People who never went through one of those, they don't know how rough it can get.

They would rather set and draw a dole. And get those food stamps. I know young guys, healthy, husky, they work long enough to draw unemployment. Then they quit. And they set and draw their unemployment.

Maybe it's their attitude that it doesn't matter, what's the use of working, we can't accomplish anything, they're going to blow up this world, one of these days. That's what's in the back of their minds, I think.

And they don't know any more about the land than they do about working. They think nature is something that they see on the television.

Some of them don't know what it is to sleep on a pine-needle bed, one of the most comfortable beds there is and a lot better smelling than a lot I've slept in. Or to take a blanket out of the pack and sleep on that. They don't know what the ground feels like. And, I think, the sophistication of camping equipment these days has a lot to do with it.

If they just could get out in the mountains, back here, in one of the primitive areas and just see what it's like to really be in nature. That might give them a different attitude.

They don't realize what a beautiful world this is. Right now. For them to enjoy, if they want to.

And they don't realize what a short time they are going to be on this earth. They don't realize that. They just don't realize.

In Bonners Ferry up in northern Idaho near the Canadian border there are hundreds of young people, refugees from California, who have taken up farming and ranching. One of the young couples who've settled there are Chris and Steve Coffman. "This is beautiful land," they said. "We wanted water and birds and trees and we wanted to be close to the mountains. We wanted dark, rich soil and we wanted wild roses and berries and mushrooms.

"And we got them all."

They said, " 'Energy' is good here. People are really working together. The land and the people on it belong together."

But there were problems in paradise. "The Californians are coming up here worth a lot of money," they said. They are driving up the land prices and are driving the local people off the land. "Now we don't tell anyone we're from California," they said.

In his spartan ranch house in the dry hills near the southern Idaho border, old Glen Sitz listened to such tales of urban homesteaders with some suspicions. He had known "hard-working hippies." And he was not opposed to anyone who worked hard, but he didn't trust the "something for nothing" people who came from California "with nothing but money" and "who played at ranching."

Those people "mostly don't really know how to work," he thought. He didn't blame them, he blamed the cities. And he squinted at the thought.

The Misfits
Glen Sitz

In the cities, they have those unemployed. Why the hell don't they come out in the country and look for a job? I will tell you. They might find something. But, to refute that, I was talking to a man the other day who was the sales manager of this business and he had a daughter, she studied sociology, or whatever the hell they call it, you know, taking care of people, and she said, and I guess it is truth, that in the cities some of those white and colored boys, they are the third generation who don't know anything.

Now, we have this third generation of young people that's grown up on that welfare. More kids think that's a way of life.

They go back and forth from one end of town to the other. Now, why the hell don't they get out into the country and root a little?

But, nowadays, the government won't let those kids work on a ranch. They're afraid they might get hurt. They're feared they might get killed. Well, I guess everybody is afraid of that. But if they don't let kids take chances, they'll never learn to do anything worthwhile.

And these kids, they got to be sixteen, and go to tractor school, before the government will let them work on a ranch. I can put them on a horse, and that could kill them, but I can't put them on a tractor. That's illegal.

And what gets me is all this yelling about kids getting in trouble in town. Hell, there's no jobs in town. But out on a ranch they won't let them work at good jobs until they're grown.

Some of them are ambitious. I used to hire a lot of kids. The last one was a big, cocky guy who was thirteen. And I was talking one day to his mother and I said, I'll do everything I can to show him what to do and I'll watch him real close and show him how to be careful. And his mother said, Well, I know that. He was a real fine hand. But that was illegal, you know.

Now we have these people who want to leave the cities, to be farmers. But if they had the chance to work on a farm I doubt if they'd be worth a damn. They have no experience. Some of them may be good. Some of them would be. But some of them are just misfit.

When I was young there was always a certain kind of people who wasn't worth a damn. In working or anything else. Now, I think, the government people they foster that.

The small town of Lander, Wyoming, has an idyllic look. For a farm and ranch community it is more prosperous than most, a neat and comfortable town, with a peaceful main street and friendly people. But looks are deceiving. The quiet town is a battlefield in what bids fair to become the range war of our century. In the countryside the power and coal companies have begun to strip-mine vast acreages of the best cattle country to unearth energy for the cities.

Some years ago one local rancher had a sense of foreboding about the coming conflict. He mortgaged his family's ranch to establish an ecology newspaper that would defend the land rights of the ranchers. He called it The High Country News.

Most folks thought that Tom Bell was a little touched. He was the third-generation rancher in his family, a sensible and respected man who had taken up with "hippies and longhairs." The local townspeople knew something wasn't right when Bell announced he was forsaking Lander and Wyoming, and going west to homestead in Oregon. Not in a covered wagon, but in a mobile home. Bell and his family went off to build a homestead ranch "with my own hands," as he said.

And he left his newspaper in the hands of a young woman from California, Joan Nice. She became its editor.

On the staff of The High Country News *there are now young people, "hippies and longhairs," from cities all over the country. Few, if any of them, have ever lived on a ranch. And yet they have dedicated themselves to "saving rural life."*

But why have they come to Lander? And what do they seek? And what do they want from the land?

"I came," said Joan Nice, "because I want to save myself."

I Was Tired of Looking in the Mirror
  Joan Nice

In this little town there is the feeling that you can shape
an island of your own making. Whether or not that has any
chance of surviving is hard to say. Now these rural areas are
receiving so much national attention. So many people are coming
out here. And in some ways the very people who want to preserve
rural life, by moving toward it, are destroying it. Because it no
longer is the same small-town way of life here, that it was before
we came out to enjoy it.

Even I, by coming here, have in some way changed the sociological stability of Lander, Wyoming. There are many people
out here, like me, who if they decided to become involved in local
politics would begin to make changes that would be alien to local
ways. And in that way we would be destroying what we came to
preserve.

Most people on our newspaper came here because they liked
the country, and the way of life. But they weren't willing to be
dishwashers; they wanted to do something meaningful. And this
is very interesting and satisfying work, trying to preserve the
American West. They came for the job, but all of them were
committed to living in a rural area in the Rockies, before they
came here for the job. It was a way of life they dreamed about.

One came from West Virginia. One came from Ohio. One
came from "the East." One came from Denver. One came from
Washington, D.C., where he had a high-pressure job putting out
the coal industry's newsletter he now opposes.

There isn't anyone here who was a rancher. Anything like
that. They are almost all kids from the cities.

For myself, the reason I am here is that I was a hiker, in California, and I discovered one of my favorite places to hike in was
about to become a Disneyland resort. So I got in touch with the
Sierra Club people who were fighting it and got interested not
only in areas, for myself, but found I was suddenly studying the
problems of oil shale and the paperwork of being a conservationist. So I came here out of self-interest.

Many of us came here for what may be called romanticism.

We were romantics. But now we are in the business of writing hard facts for rural people so that they can preserve their own way of life.

In a rural area like this it's hard for people to get the information which they need to determine their own destiny. And this newspaper is one way of getting the facts out to them that will arm them for the fight that we see as crucial to this region. That fight is for the natural resources of the West.

And, in doing that, I feel that I've become a part of this community. Now this is my home. This is my small town. This is where I want to live. This is where I want to stay.

Nothing could make me move now. I have become part of this way of life, and it has become part of me.

On the day I sat in the old general store of the ghost town of Shakespear and talked with Rita and Janaloo Hill, my admiring eyes were drawn to some photographs on the wall behind the potbelly stove. They were of a beautiful woman, posed in the manner of a high-fashion model. She looked hauntingly familiar.

And suddenly it dawned on me that they were photographs of Janaloo. Maybe twenty years younger.

Yes, she smiled. Those photographs had been taken in New York City, when she had gone to be on Broadway, the Great White Way. She had wanted to make her mark in the big city, as so many rural youth had always done. And though she had accomplished more than most, she had come home quicker than most.

Why had she gone? And why had she returned?

"Sometimes it's good to get away so you can know if you really want to stay," she said. "It's sometimes necessary to lose something before you can be aware of what you've lost."

Am I Happy I Went Away?
Janaloo Hill

Am I happy that I went away, went to New York? Oh, yes.

If I didn't I would feel cheated. So I had to go. To see. To learn what it might be like to be on Broadway. On the stage. For a while I was a dancer in the ballet and in the chorus, and in shows and all that. In many ways I liked New York. And I still miss a great many things in the city.

But I am glad to be back on the ranch.

Here I hope I can make a contribution to life that I probably couldn't in the world of the theater. The ghost town of Shakespear, New Mexico, needs me. The ghost of Shakespeare in New York doesn't. The theater in New York can get along, I am sure, quite well without me.

And the ways it's going I am just as glad to be out of show business; it is getting grubbier by the day.

Maybe I feel that we should contribute something to life, not just to ourselves. We are only here a little while on earth. One human being can make only such an infinitesimal contribution in any case. But we have to try. Sometimes yelling about an injustice, such as ranchers face, is an important thing.

So I don't feel I have retreated, hidden myself from life, out here on the ranch. I feel I am more a part of living than I was in New York.

Do I miss dancing? Well, cows don't dance.

There aren't too many opportunities for dancers out in this part of the country. Although there are more now than there used to be when I was younger.

And I keep up my interest in dancing. Springtime we put up a show here in this ghost town with the children from up in Lordsburg as the dancers. I teach them. Ballet. Modern. Jazz. And we make all our own costumes and I do the choreography.

For whom? Ourselves. It's a world of dance just for us. It's the ghost town dance theater.

In that biblical rhetoric that he loved to imitate, the nine-teenth-century poet Henry Wadsworth Longfellow once asked of those who had gone from the country to the city, as if accusing them of betraying the land:

How canst thou who hast trod
the prairies,
Walk the streets of the city?

But the folks from the rural West were less troubled by that feat than the poet from the urban East.

From the beginning many of the settlers of the West had come from the cities of the East. And ever since, the cities of the West had been mostly populated by the sons and daughters of these settlers. The migration from urban to rural and back again from rural to urban had been circular, like the cycles of the seasons and the cycles of history.

In that, America was unique.

And yet not many people had traveled the full circle. Roberta Cheney and her children had done so. She and they had all gone from the family's homesteading ranch, which went back five generations, to the cities, where they had lived, and the universities, where they taught, and then back home once again. Like homing pigeons.

That was not what she and her husband had planned. When they retired they had thought, at first, of buying a condominium apartment, by the sea. And here they were on the family ranch in Montana, somewhat to their wonderment.

Even when they settled, quietly and happily, into her child-hood home, they could not help but wonder. Just what was it that "pulls one back home"?

Going Home Again
Roberta Cheney

And you ask: Why did I come back to the ranch?

One thing that brought us back to the ranch is our beautiful mountains; we like the mountains; we like to look out of our windows and see the high Rocky Mountains. It is not only inspiring. It is comforting. And we feel protected by these mountains, from the world outside of our valley.

I think we gain a strength from these mountains.

There was no feeling of strength of that kind when we were living in the cities. No city can give you that sense of comfort that mountains can give you. And the peace.

When I left the valley it was because I had to, to go to high school. Because there wasn't even a high school in the valley. Then I went to college and I married and I taught in universities and I didn't really think of coming home to the ranch, to live.

And fifty years later, when we retired, we decided that of all these places we had been this was the place we wanted to live. So we came home again.

Now, we are sort of back to the kind of living I grew up with. Except that now there isn't the hard work there once was, because we have the money to have what we want and we don't have a debt hanging over our head, which I remember always from the early days.

You know, I am not around a theater. Not around a university. Not around those big city stores. But I feel I can drive to those things, if I want to. And I have all my books. And I feel I am not "out of it" even though I live in the country.

And I don't feel isolated. The way I once did.

In the winter we are never really snowed in. The school bus comes by. And the rural mail delivery comes by three times a week. And that's enough. That's just about plenty.

But there is something else. Something more important.

When our oldest daughter, Karen, was married, we were living in Portland. But she chose for her wedding not one of the big cathedrals which we attended in Portland, but the little rural church down in Jeffers, Montana, which is a tiny, little old white-frame Episcopalian Church. She had been baptized in the church. She came back to be married here.

There is something that pulls one back home. And, if we can, we always want to come home again.

"Time went to sleep here and everything fell dreaming. . . .

"As I sit here in this place of knowing silence, I close my eyes and days no longer move, and all the years exist together. I can see my old Grandfather as he was here, with his long brown beard and bright blue eyes—young and brisk. And I can see my old Grandmother the way she was years after Pa was gone, rocking restlessly in her chair. And I can hear her saying, with the glow of remembered happiness on her withered face: 'Oh, John, if I could only be in our covered wagon again, going West with Pa and the babies!' "

The passage is from that wonderful memory of his pioneering family by John G. Neihardt, author of Black Elk Speaks. *He entitled it wisely,* All Is But the Beginning.

On his family homestead he was not haunted by his memories of history. He was part of that history. It lived not only in his memories, but in the place itself. The house and the trees and the land gave his memories a physical presence and form—as if the past were the present. For there is a sense of history that we get from having a place on earth that we do not get from man-made things.

Sons and daughters of the homesteaders who go back to the old place have often had that experience. It sometimes disturbs them. It sometimes troubles them. For in a time that seems uprooted, where speed is God, and people pride themselves on living day by day, the unyielding embrace of history may be unnerving.

Bill Kitteridge, the son of a rancher, not only lived in, but had tried to recreate that sense of history. He did it by doing what I am doing, writing it down.

One evening in a bar in Great Falls, Montana, I encountered Kitteridge by accident. I had gone there to meet his girl friend for my book. Soon I was conscious of a large and gregarious man who seemed to be talking to everyone in the bar, at once. He reminded me of Thomas Wolfe.

Later, in a motel room, Bill recorded his thoughts on eternity and ranching, interrupted only by the rumble of the diesel trucks passing on the highway.

The Landscapes of Our Minds
Bill Kitteridge

One time I went home to the little town where I grew up, in this valley, and I ran into an Irish guy, a wonderful guy I used to know. One night we were in this bar where I hadn't been in ten years. And he started telling stories; he loved to talk. He started bellyaching about all the things changing in the valley, how the valley was no longer ours, how everything was mechanical. And he starts talking about "Tokyo quarter horses."

Well, I didn't know what a "Tokyo quarter horse" was.

He says: It's a Honda!

And we all rode on horseback before and now we ride Hondas. So it's still the same energies, the same life, the same ethos. Things are not really destroyed; they are not really gone. In a different way they become the same sort of things. They are just another version of the same things. I believe we are not really different from the way we grew up.

Th environment is different. And in ten thousand years or one hundred thousand years, we may be different. But not in seventy-five years.

People in the valley where I grew up, it seems to me they are still living there and they are still comfortable living there. Most of them go on doing whatever they did. Go to town. Go to the store. Go visiting. And they just go on as they did before.

Oh, hell! Someone may build a house of Styrofoam in the valley. But, so what? It doesn't matter. People still make love and have children and tell stories in Styrofoam houses.

And there's nothing really all that wrong with life in the valley. It's just a little more ironic.

To ride in a car, which is a metal box, and to play country-western music on the radio, is unnatural. Because that music tells you nine emotional lies every second and then the ad comes on and it tells you more lies and you look up at the billboards by the roadside and they tell you more lies. It is unnatural to be told that many lies constantly about where you are, in the West, and who you are, a human being in the West.

Now, it's gotten so that I'm not at all certain that a tree on television isn't just as real as a real tree. It's not easy to see if we are real or not.

So a lot of us who grew up in the West, I think, have given up. Really in a cynical and bad sort of way. To us it may seem that our world has completely changed and it is never going to be as it was when I was a child. Never. The place that I grew up in had a million and a quarter acres. And you can't imagine how big that desert was.

On the old maps it said: This is the Great American Desert. And that was the real frontier.

Now, I don't go crazy in that environment. I throw rocks at it. If you were to see someone walking in the grasslands and throwing rocks at rabbits you wouldn't say he is crazy, would you? But, you know, I grew up in the reality of the West, and not in the fantasy.

And I am not at all sure that it is possible for me to maintain the whole business of living in two worlds. Personally. Of going back to the valley from the city, two or three times a year. And the rest of the time hiding out in the city; I'm not sure that is possible. But, I know I do that.

Meanwhile the people I know in the city, who have lived in the city all their lives, they go out to my valley, looking for something, and demanding that it be as they imagine it to be. They have a structured vision of how things should be that they impose on people in the valley. That they should live in log cabins like those prefabricated log cabins they're building for themselves. And they should wear spurs on their jogging shoes in the bars.

This is how I see it:

In the landscapes of our minds, we have to learn how we can

make a place for ourselves. And we are going increasingly to learn how to do that, because our outside worlds are going continually to be destroyed.

These kinds of changes are something we have to learn to live with, to work with, to do with, to transform into something that we can value. I see absolutely no point in restoration of the past.

And things will not be like they were. Of course. They can't possibly be like they were because they never were like they were in the first place.

So, to me, the thing is not to give in, to accept, a false idea of ourselves. But to make things be the way we would have them be. To me the West is not dead. It doesn't have to be dead.

But I am much less interested in the world's view of me than in my own past. It is still alive in my head. Even though it's not there anymore—it is. The valley I grew up in was full of horses. And in my head the horses are still there, though they are not really there.

I hear them! I hear them!

And so, I grew up in a very different world and in this world I feel like a very, very old man.

That's because the past is alive in all of us.

And Thou
Art Cursed
Above All Cattle

9

Stay on the Ranch? Shit, No!
Gerald Allen

Me? Do I want to stay on the ranch? Shit, no!

If I was back in the cities I would have just as much independence and just as much fresh air, standing on some street
corner, as here. And I'd have a lot more peace of mind.

So why did I come back?

For some time I been boondocking around the country. Was
damn near drinking myself to death. And I knew I had to quit
that. So I come back and I been here near fourteen years now.

My dad took this place right where we're settin' out of grease-
wood and sagebrush. As a kind of rough guess I'd say my dad
came here, let me see, if he was alive he'd be around a hundred
and four, or something like that. And he came here when he
was about twenty-five. So, I'd say, he came here in 1902. Or,
something like that.

There was no water on this side of the river then. Just brush.
And dad put this ranch here. He made it.

I was born and raised here. And I stayed here until I was
twenty years old. Then I left. Was gone for, oh, about twenty-
five years. My brother run the place. And he got killed in a
truck wreck. Then a year or so later my dad died. And they was
going to sell the place. And I guess I had more sentiment than
sense. And so, I came back.

For twenty-five years I hoboed around the country. While my
family kept this place going. So maybe I keep at it in apprecia-

tion. And since I come back home this place has more than doubled in dollar worth. And I have upped that with improvements. Besides my mother, if I was to leave, she'd hemorrhage.

But the economics of ranching is impossible now. And just as soon as I can get loose from here, I will.

The old-time method of operation was keep your overhead down. Whatever you produced was profit. That's how they looked at it. And in those days the help was loyal.

Nowadays you can't hire any hands because no one knows how to work a ranch anymore. So you got to put in thirty-six hours a day teaching them. And then the next day they're gone. To hell with them. You got to do it all almost yourself.

On this ranch I have a fellow who had to sell his own ranch he inherited, to pay the debts and taxes. But, shit, he ain't worth much; he's just lost most of his spirit.

So, I have this sign on the wall of my kitchen: ANYONE WHO ENJOYS WORKING—CAN CERTAINLY HAVE A HELL OF A TIME ON THIS PLACE

No, it's bad diplomacy, that sign. I should turn it to the wall.

That's a pretty gloomy, pessimistic perspective on ranching. But it's not near as bad as I think. It could be a hell of a lot worse.

So, why do I stay in ranching?

Well, on the other hand, it's a nice life. You got a great diversity in your work. It'll challenge you from here right to hell. On a ranch you got to be a lawyer and diplomat and agronomist and veterinarian. And a shit shoveler!

Now, being a truck driver or a cat skinner or a banker, I been all of those. But you just got to have some activity you got some incentive in. And I think that basically the ranching way of life is superior. It is like Eisenhower used to say, that without the American family our nation would have no backbone. And I feel that way about agriculture; it don't have to necessarily be ranching, but I could be raising sugar beets.

Hell, I don't know. In this advanced civilization we got to have lawyers and cars, I guess. But we could get along without them. Fundamentally we can't get along without agriculture.

My dream?

I want to get enough acreage down in southwest Oregon to run about two hundred sheep. Perfect sheep. I want to get an animal that's a five-way cross of the Finn, for multiple births, and the Rambalain, for mothering ability, and the Lincoln for size, and the coarser wool of the Panama and the Black-face, for a thick coat.

And with those two hundred perfect sheep, I could spend half my time there and be gone half the time. Off fishing and to go hunting, or whatever it happens to be. That's enough to keep me occupied without busting my back. And to give me some income to live on.

So I can go to San Francisco? Hell, no! Two nights there is enough for me.

The line of tall trees along the road to the house gave the place an old and comfortable look of a peasant village in France. Even the house with its wide porches had a usually lived-in and leisurely atmosphere about it, which suggested an old and large family. And the garden gate, made of dozens of old-style horseshoes welded together in an intricate design, resembled a sort of ancestral family crest.

But the house was empty. The rancher, Gerald Allen, lived there alone.

In the ranch house the faded curtains were drawn. From the way they looked they had been drawn for years. A dim light that filtered through the curtains cast a dustlike shadow on the piles of newspapers and books and unopened letters that were scattered about on the tables and chairs and floor.

On the kitchen sink there seemed to be more dishes than were on the shelves. And the ashtray on the kitchen table was filled with more cigarette butts than flies on a hog.

The mess reminded me of farm kitchens I had known during the Depression. Somehow I felt at home.

And as we sat at his kitchen table and talked, I thought that this rancher's litany of laments fit with his surroundings. The curses that he placed upon the world, he placed as well upon himself; he not only protested it, he gloried in it.

On that summer day, in spite of his talk of doom, the ranch looked just fine. The grass was tall. The cattle were fat. In the trees the locusts were sassy. And there was a cool breeze. For all of his cursing, that was the world, the only world, he really loved and wanted.

None of the hardships of ranching that he talked about were new to him. Or to any rancher.

That was the way life had always been on a ranch. That was the way it always would be. One might say that if it was not that way, ranching never would have been ranching at all.

Ranchers did not really expect to overcome the hardships of life. Because by next summer or next winter they always came back again, as surely as one season followed another. And these hardships defined ranch life, shaped its character, and gave it meaning.

No rancher's lament ever expressed it better than the re-markable story of Ruth and Tug Pettit. They remembered not one, but four, ranches that had been lost in the odyssey of their families' wanderings across the West.

And yet they told of all these defeats and failures with a laconic enthusiasm for ranching. It was simply the way life was for any rancher, where death and birth were natural, and to be expected, and when it happened you made-do somehow, you kept going, you began anew.

They just "sort of endured some way," they said.

Lost Every Damn Thing We Had
Tug and Ruth Pettit

TUG: Sold out in 1918. My dad, he finally had to sell out. Got beat out of everything. Lost everything. He sold out to an oil fellow. He had to take stock in this well and that well. For the ranch. They'd show him a producing well, but when it came down to brass tacks, his stock was in nothing but dry holes. My dad got a lawyer. But they bought the lawyer off. One law-yer, they claimed, can't put another lawyer on the stand in court.

We lost every damn thing we had!

And when my mother died she left us a section of the ranch. But the compounded taxes on it were more than we could sell it for. So we told a friend to take it off'n our hands.

Now there's oil on it!

RUTH : On my mother's grandfather's place there are now two oil wells in the feedlot. He died in 1900. He tried to put things in each of his kids' names. And I don't know how they finagled them out of it. But when my grandfather and father died, Mother sold the ranch. And Mother did not know she could hold the mineral rights, because we had no idea then that there was anything to hold onto. So she lost all her mineral rights.

And we lost everything.

TUG : When my dad sold out the fellow bought most of the livestock. My dad kept three milk cows and a team of mules. And us boys kept our best saddle horses.

The boys all scattered. Because we was all old enough to go on our own. Dad loaded up and moved off. He give the fellow possession. He trusted him. But that fellow never did come across with even the down payment; just kept putting dad off.

So dad give him thirty days. When the thirty days were up he come and asked for thirty more. It was supposed to be for $65,000, over the barrel head. Never did get it. But that fellow done got possession, you see. And Dad, he couldn't do nothing.

That fellow he shipped all the cattle out as quick as he could. And he hired me to do it. He thought I was my uncle's boy. But I kept a record of it. And so we wrangled around it for eleven years after. But we never did get any money.

All of us had houses and cultivation on that ranch. But when the court finally settled it, he had rented everything out to cotton farmers. They were stealing people.

That's when we went down south Texas, to ranch there. And I bought a fellow out down there. And that's when the grasshoppers came in and cleaned us out. Everywhere you went there were grasshoppers underfoot. Some places, inches thick, of them grasshoppers.

RUTH : I would have crawled to get out of Texas.

TUG : That was when we decided to get our stock together,

what was left, and we made these covered wagons and we went over the mountains, alookin' for a home, just goin' west.

And that's what we did. That was in 1932. Like I said, they told us we was the last wagon train west.

But I doubt it. Someone else's always goin' to come along.

On rough roads that are more like horse trails, in the backcountry, beyond the hills, the scrawny homestead ranches of many an old-timer are hidden away. They have survived that way. That may well be because so few outsiders have been able to find these out-of-the-way places. So far. And it may be because the old-time ranches are mostly too small and poor to interest the outside world, til now.

And so the small homesteaders, who survived homesteading, often still do.

But the big ranches of the cattle barons of old have largely vanished into history. The legendary spreads with their vast herds have become myths. Gone are the Matador, the XIT, the Miller Lux, the Peter French, the Powder River, the Goodnight, and all the rest.

Some of these ranches, like the Matador, were run by absentee owners in foreign countries, from the start. There were Russian princes, French counts, German barons, English lords, and Scottish merchants who owned much of the West. By 1883, the president of the Colorado Cattle Growers' Association said these foreigners "would eventually own and control the bulk of the cattle interests in the country."

The family of William Lumpkin came west, in the 1880s, to work as wranglers on the old Matador Ranch. One of his uncles was a foreman there. Even then the Matador was owned by these Scottish bankers and investors whose ranching decisions were based more on the doings of the stock exchanges than on the cows.

So too, when the Lumpkins established their own ranches of more than a quarter of a million acres in New Mexico and Arizona, their success or failure was determined by brokerage as much as by ranching standards. They had so much money in-

vested in their huge herds that when the beef prices rose and
fell in the cities the ranch rose and fell with them.
And the Lumpkins, like the Pettits, lost everything they had.

Land Rich, but Money Poor
William Lumpkin

The cattle industry has never been the romantic barons-of-the-West sort of thing in this country.

Ranchers, independent ranchers, always had hard times. Because the rancher has never controlled the market for beef in the East. He's got no say. That's how we lost both our ranches, the big one in Arizona and the one in Lincoln County. We just lost near everything, because of what happened after World War I.

Because in World War I they created a tremendous demand for beef. And everybody built up their herds and overextended themselves. Then suddenly, after the war, prices of beef just plummeted downward, you know. There wasn't the demand in relation to the supply. You get high beef prices during wars and low beef demand after wars. It's always up and down.

And so, depression hit the cattle industry. There were banks broke all over the Southwest. Like in Roswell, there were five banks there, and four of them failed, and in Albuquerque, I think, there was six or seven bank failures.

My father lost the Arizona ranch. He still held on to the Lincoln County ranch. He was land rich, but money poor.

One year I remember Dad got a job in town, driving a mail truck, just to pay the taxes on the damn ranch. Mother would raise chickens and sell them. But there never was enough cash.

Depression! It didn't really impress us kids, because you're not really geared to the economy of money when you're young. Sometimes when we'd go to town and stay in town for three days, we'd be given a quarter. And that was supposed to last for the three days we were in town. And it did.

So, we didn't really think about that Depression then. But I do now.

On a summer day, standing beneath the huge trees that shade the ranch house, and gazing across the endless plains to the distant mountains, one had the feeling that one was alone; alone with whatever gods there may be. There was a sense of natural serenity and of personal peace that existed on such a ranch. Nothing that I had ever experienced equaled that feeling of oneness with the world.

The Stephenson ranch was surrounded by such solitary splendor. It was unbelievably beautiful.

Even so, the ranch was not all that different from any other. It was not more or less beautiful, nor more or less peaceful. The natural world of a ranch, however distinctive and unique, almost always seemed to cast that sort of calming and soothing spell on a visitor.

And yet Billy Stephenson, in the midst of the splendid isolation and quiet of his ranch, felt crowded. He could feel the government bureaucrats breathing down his neck, he said, from the other side of these mountains, thousands of miles away. It was a nightmare he had. They were looking over his shoulder. They watched his every step. They regulated everything he did.

In the setting of these mountains and plains Stephenson's complaint seemed absurd, if not paranoid. But, he insisted, "Ranching most likely is the most regulated business in the country," and it was no longer "free like it was."

Maybe it was so. Maybe it was not. Maybe it was simply the contrast between the aloneness of a rancher's life, his sense of solitude and individualism, and the world of bureaucratic labyrinths, which made him feel persecuted by those things that most people just accepted as part of life in the twentieth century.

From Montana to New Mexico, in any event, the complaint of ranchers I talked with was the same as Stephenson's lament. He merely expressed his anger with more wry humor.

There's a Jillion Different Biddy Laws
    Billy Stephenson

Ranchers may say they like ranching because they're their own bosses. But it's really not too much like that anymore. Oh, if you want to go out there and fix fence, you can, or if you want to lay under a tree, you can. More or less up to you. Far as work goes, that's right. You do what you want to. You can go let your cows die, or you can go feed them. That's up to you.

But, what we do on the land, we're pretty well controlled by the government. You are not really your own boss.

Nowadays it seems like all of our troubles come from something the government does. They affect us in just about every thing we do. Like all the restrictions they have on our using federal and state lands. Like after they passed that Wild Horses and Burros Act, it seems like, why, it would get to the point where we'd be running as many wild horses and burros as we were cattle. The rancher leases a little federal land to run cattle on it, and make a little money, and they come and say we're going to cut your cattle herd fifty percent and we're going to run the other fifty percent in wild horses and burros, why, we can't make a living on that.

Or, like they tell you: you can't feed your cattle this kind of feed, you got to feed that kind instead. Or, like you can't fix this fence up, without taking off the bottom wire off. Or, like you can't put that gate on your corral, because the wild burros don't know how to open it.

There's a jillion different biddy laws like that. A lot of them I don't even know about.

And we are going to have to live by them. Because if we don't we can't go on ranching on federal lands. Even though those are our lands too.

Lord knows how many meetings I have been to around the country, where we complained about these regulations. But it's always after the regulation's been written in Washington. And trying to get one changed is pretty hard to do. We're just a few ranchers and the government's got millions of other people, who never been on a ranch, backing them. They don't even know what it is they're backing and what it does.

Once we had advisory boards to the Bureau of Land Management that we elected local people and ranchers to. And that was good. But, even then, the laws were written down in Washington. Not here.

The laws are then sent down here and these local bureau people, their job is just to enforce them and tell you what to do. All they are is just yes-men for the bureaucrats in Washington. So they've got no more say than we do.

Because of those laws the coyotes are increasing and the cattle are decreasing. They are more interested in protecting the coyotes than they are in protecting the cattle and sheep. And I think the increasing coyotes have been killing the young antelope. So they'll probably be passing a new law.

Maybe there's one way to kill the coyotes and the laws. That's if enough of these Washington bureaucrats were to move out here and build summer homes and saw what their laws do.

That would be something.

Nothing symbolized the conflict between the ranchers and the government more clearly than "The Battle of the Barbed Wire." Someone, somewhere, somehow, in some government office, issued a regulation that ordered that the bottom wire of any barbed-wire fence had to be sixteen to eighteen inches above the ground. One rancher cynically said that the regulation was aimed at protecting "predators and coyotes so that they could go from one pasture to another without stooping, or scratching their backs."

And he was right.

By ordering the barbed wire to be high enough so coyotes could easily crawl under it, the Bureau of Land Management of the U.S. Department of Interior was doing what was required by federal law. The urban environmentalists wished to protect the wild animals. And the rural environmentalists wished to protect their nonwild animals, the lambs and calves. It was a classic conflict between urban and rural views. And, as usual, the government enforced the law of the democratic majority.

Ranchers were a tiny minority. Even the laws written to govern their lives seemed to them to be written by those who opposed their way of life.

The Roman philosopher Cicero stated the ranchers' position some time ago: "The produce of the earth was solely designed for those who make use of it and if some beasts rob us of a small part of it that does not mean that the earth produced it for them."

Evidently, the Bureau of Land Management did not agree. Its order concerning coyotes had to do with more than coyotes, for two very different ways of viewing life were in conflict. And to the ranchers the government had become their opposition.

"Some ranchers are so hostile to the Bureau of Land Management. They hate them. They are the enemy," one rancher said. "Not realizing the enemy is something much bigger; it is not the little man who comes out in a pickup to enforce these idiotic laws that come out of Washington."

In the ways that Gerald Allen and Madlyn Cauhape and her son saw it, the "enemy" was large indeed. The rest of the entire country seemed to be the "enemy" and they did not like it at all. Everyone was against them. And they stood alone, misunderstood, insulted, abused, humiliated, demeaned and, worst of all, ignored.

That seemed to be the message in Gerald Allen's "The Coyote, the Son of a Bitch" and Madlyn and Marion Cauhape's "They Cut Our Fences."

It was more than coyotes that they feared.

The Coyote, the Son of a Bitch
Gerald Allen

On calfing time out here we put in fourteen hours a day. On horseback. We go out with rifles. In spite of that coyotes get one or two calves a day. They'll watch a cow and they will know when she's going to calf. And when she lays down and starts kicking the calf out, the coyote, the son of a bitch, he kills the calf even before it's born. Sometime he waits. And when the newborn calf starts getting up on its legs, the coyotes will eat it alive. They begin eating on its ass until he's eaten.

One time two old sheep got out of the fence and I couldn't get them back in. So I thought those goddamn bastards, let the coyotes get them. And then a bunch of sheep began following those two old sheep. But the coyotes never touched them. They didn't know what sheep was. All they knew was calves.

Sometime people don't know why we feel the way we do about coyotes. There ain't too many coyotes in New York.

Remember this lady who was out to protect the gopher? She was a damn good writer. And she made the ranchers sound like the cruelest, inhuman bastards who ever existed, since ancient times, 'cause they poisoned gophers. Well, to most people the gopher is just a cute little animal. And the same applies to a coyote, as they see it.

And if I didn't know the coyote, as I do, I'd have to admit he is a beautiful animal.

And when you see the coyotes back here on the mountain, with his head back, howling, that's romantic. But when I see that son of a bitch eating a calf alive and killing lambs, eighteen or twenty in a bunch, just for the sake of killing, well, it takes the beauty out of it.

No way that a coyote can ever be beautiful to me.

They Cut Our Fences
Madlyn and Marion Cauhape

MOTHER: People don't realize that our wildlife won't be here if it weren't for the ranchers. We put out the protein blocks just the other day and the wildlife they eat it just like the stock do. And, we put out salt for the livestock and the wildlife eat that just like our stock do. Then we put in thirteen wells on our ranch and miles and miles of pipelines, so our livestock can utilize the grass better and the wildlife they drink that water too.

On this ranch right here, the river runs through it. And we got one seep in the backcountry. But other than that it is just flash floods when it rains. It's our windmills that supply water for that wildlife.

Now, they want more wildlife so the hunters can come and kill it. And so the eastern people can come in and tear up our rangeland while looking for wildlife and recreation.

SON: One time they said that we'd been messing up the habitat for all those little birdies and things that these eastern hunters hunt. So they came out to our ranch with a list of regulations that was the stupidest crap I ever heard in my life. We had a road at the bottom of the canyon back in here and they wanted us to put the road up on top of the ridge. Why? No reason that I know.

And they wanted us to go and take up all our water troughs and pick them up and move them. But we got these big old concrete and steel dudes and you couldn't move them. But they wanted them moved. And they wanted those water troughs set on ground level so all the little rats, and stuff, they could get a drink of water. And they wanted an escape ramp built into those water troughs so those little varmints if they fell in the water, they could get out.

If we did that, those water troughs would be full of mud all the time. Tumbleweeds and mud. And our livestock they'd have to drink mud.

MOTHER: But they don't care much about our livestock. They care more about predators.

SON: Back in the spring, when we'd had lambs everywhere, I got a call one afternoon. And it was someone up the road, here. And he had just seen two coyotes, arunning across the road not two miles up from our turnoff here. Two coyotes ran across the road in front of him. You see at lambing time in the spring you move heaven and earth to get at those coyotes before they get at your lambs and calves. We will call all the neighbors and they will come with horses and pickups and all the shotguns they got. 'Cause it gives us fits.

So I called this foreman of this outfit over here. And he said, this rancher, he don't live on that ranch, he was just a dude, and he don't want to bother with raising sheep and he didn't want us to kill those coyotes on his ranch. That those coyotes were going to raise fifty or sixty little coyotes and that they're going to wander all over and give everybody fits, didn't matter to him.

And so we had to take airplanes up. He didn't own the sky.

MOTHER: These eastern people get the idea, well, they're all God's creatures. But God gave man dominion over the animals. And, I think, we need a little bit more dominion, if those eastern people are going to eat and we ranchers are going to survive.

SON: I wonder, did any of them ever eat coyote?

MOTHER: Or want to?

SON: They don't hardly ever try to understand what ranching is. And why we need fences to keep coyotes out just like banks need to keep robbers out.

MOTHER: Most of this country wasn't fenced until the 1930s.

And you need good fences for good sheep. Because you got your bucks in one pasture and you don't want them all over the country. You want to have some control over your bucks' habits. And you need good fences so you can keep the coyotes out, so you can have a good lamb crop and not let the coyotes get your lambs.

Then these government people come in and tell us we can't have fences like that because the antelope have to migrate to survive. And the fences interfere with the antelope migration. Here, where there never has been an antelope habitat. So they come in and cut some of our fences. They cut our sheep-proof fences. And they put in three or four barbed-wire fences. And the bottom wire, they put that sixteen inches off the ground. Why, that's just opening the gate for all the predators and coyotes and varmints.

And you can't keep your bucks separated when you got that kind of a fence; it'll just kill any kind of breeding program you might want to do. Neighbor sheep can just wander through. And they mess up your sheep's bloodlines.

If you don't do it right they're down your collar. Oh, you can talk to them, you can fuss with them, but when it comes right down to the bottom line, about the only thing you can do to try to protect your property rights is to take the government to court.

Can you imagine that our own government goes onto private property, and cuts our fences? They wouldn't be doing that to a factory fence.

On this fencing business it's the Bureau of Land Management people who are going out there and cutting these fences. So it's not as if they just told the ranchers to do it. They're doing it themselves.

And they propagate themselves with all these rules and regulations. Not many years ago the local manager of the bureau office had two or three secretaries. Now there are seventy-five people in that bureau office.

Then they bring in college kids. I don't have anything against college kids except they have no experience in ranching. And they don't understand our situation, because a book says so and so is so.

So we are not ruled in our lives by the people we elect. But by the bureaucrats. They write the regulations and that's what we live by, the regulations, not the laws. And when they have more of the city people than rural people in the government offices it's just hard to make ourselves heard. We're such a minority. There are so many of them. And even when we are heard I just don't know the right thing to say to reach them. You see, it's these other people, the government people, who are forcing us ranchers out of business.

They decide what we do. And we can holler and buck all we want.

I remember the day that I first met Rita Hill. She was sitting on a folding chair, bundled up against the wind, in front of the state capital buildings, all by herself; an old lady appealing to the governor and the legislators who passed her by. And she was holding a sign which read something like this:

PLEASE HELP ME SAVE MY RANCH
FROM THE BULLDOZERS OF THE INTERSTATE HIGHWAY

Most passersby thought she was a crazy old woman, as they said. A fool. A kook.

But her appeal seemed logical and rational enough to me. The interstate highway was being built through her home town of Lordsburg, and an interchange was planned in the middle of one of her cow pastures. And for nearly one year Rita Hill halted that interstate highway.

She did it not merely by protesting, but by building a shack in her pastures, in the path of the bulldozers and by moving into it. One old lady defying the multibillion-dollar highway system. She did stop the machines. But in the end the interstate highway rolled over her. The bulldozers pulled down her shack. Her cows had to find another pasture.

She became a legend. A folk heroine of sorts. One day her deeds probably will be sung and resung as a symbol of the independent spirit of the West.

But Rita Hill was no legend. She was just a rancher trying to save one of her good pastures.

My Cows Didn't Need That Highway
Rita Hill

My cows, the way I reasoned, didn't need that interchange on the interstate highway right in the middle of their pasture.

So I fought it. I fought it and I went to jail to stop it. I fought it up in the state capital, all by myself. But no one would listen to me. I fought it by building that shack right in the path of that interstate. My God! It was going to go through my land, my cow pasture. And so, I fought it, all by myself.

Many people they don't stay with things long enough. I stayed with that until the land was destroyed. And there was no use anymore. There was no use for me to stay in jail any longer. Because they destroyed the land as soon as they had me off of it. The sheriff, he was ashamed at first to arrest me. An old woman. Now, after all, how would that look? But, they forced him to do it.

An interstate highway, that's more important than an old woman. Isn't it? So, I lost my fight.

Even the construction company for the highway didn't really want to build that interchange. They didn't approve of the plans for that highway, but they had to do what the contract called for. They are friends of mine now. And then the highway department began trying to be nice to me. They offered me money.

So I decided I was being selfish. Because we couldn't pay our grazing fees and it was a great worry to my daughter, she works so hard with the cattle, I decided to accept the money on behalf of the ranch. Not myself.

This is a very small ranch. It is very insignificant. Now, we're not of any importance at all, we're very small, poor people. And we don't amount to much. No one cares about us.

And two years ago we couldn't pay our grazing fees, we just couldn't possibly pay them. Well, when that highway department allowed me so much money for the land they took away, at first I wouldn't accept it. But the highway department had cut off water on that pasture where the highway was and we couldn't run our cattle down there on our own land. So I accepted the money and we piped water down there from this windmill we have up here. And we paid our grazing fees. And we put in two new wells.

Even though I thought that interchange they wanted to build in my cows' pasture was a silly thing. It just wasn't needed. They tore up our pasture, all our grass, all our vegetation. If you tear up the vegetation in this desert it isn't going to come back in your lifetime. We don't have enough rain.

And they paid me for doing that. For doing that to my land.

Now, a lot of people thought that I was a crazy old woman for fighting that. But who was really crazy?

One thing that ranchers seemed to have in common, if little else, was a sense of place, a place on earth. It was not so much that they owned a place on earth, though that had something to do with it, but that the place on earth they owned was where their ancestors were buried, where they grew up and would die, and where their children were born.

They were part of that earth. And their feeling came from more than simply owning, buying, and selling the earth. It went deeper.

So, when a rancher like Wallace McRae of the Rocker Six Cattle Company began talking about what his land meant to him, he suddenly sounded sentimental and romantic. He insisted he was not. He was a practical, down-to-earth sort of man. He was "no idealist about a piece of damned Montana dirt."

But, to those whose roots are what they see on television, McRae might seem romantic indeed. He spoke of the earth as if it was part of his family. And he spoke of the coal companies who waited for him to sell his land, as if they were rapists in his bedroom. "Locusts," he said.

And he held his roots in the dirt in his hands.

To Be a Tough Hand
Wallace McRae

No, I cannot see any compatibility between the cattle business and the energy business. Some people say that I can stay here and run a cow outfit while they strip-mine for coal. I don't think that's possible. But let's say it is. Let's say that my psyche could take that and that I could ride by a damn mine on my horse, every day, and not be bothered. Let's say that you need a certain amount of acres, that I am willing to set aside, for your mines, say two thousand acres.

Okay?

Should I give them my horse pasture? What is going to be my mode of transportation when I go around in the spring and fall and round up my cows? And so, I don't think I can give them my horse pasture. And I can't give them my meadows. Several months out of the year I depend upon the production of those meadows to feed my cattle through the winter. And I don't think I can give them my bull pasture, because I'm not going to be able to clip any coupons off of those bulls unless I use them to breed. Maybe they want part of my winter pasture, well, that messes up my summer pasture.

And so maybe I should take part of my summer pasture and part of my winter pasture and give them an equal amount of both. But that isn't going to be an efficient mining unit, because they aren't adjacent to one another.

Maybe they want my heifer pasture or my pasture where I calf out my two-year-old heifers. But I need that too, because otherwise if I have to pull a calf I wouldn't have them close in enough to the house to do that logistically. And I need those pastures nearby.

So the problem I have with this is that I can't see a logical place for a mining unit on my outfit that meets the logic of my cattle business, as well. Where am I going to get those two thousand acres?

My ranch, I feel, is a well-balanced geographic and economic unit. Everything fits together. It's almost an isolated ecosystem of its own. And what part of this ecosystem can I do without, for one year, for five years?

None at all. On my ranch I really grow energy, that's what grasses and cows really are. Energy. But that depends upon its ecosystem, which has to stay intact. Has to be whole.

Civilized mankind has always eaten up the principal of the earth and we haven't used the interest of the earth, and preserved the principal. We are always digging and digging and digging into the principal. And that's what we are doing now. We are not using the interest. There is energy interest that comes from the sun every day. And we don't use that. No, we have to dig up and use the principal, which is the coal, which is the oil, which is not the grass, which is not the animals.

And I am opposed to that. That's maybe why I am a rancher.

Oh, I get tired of fighting those windmills. I get tired of fighting the winter. I get tired of fighting the grasshoppers. But, I turned out to be a tough hand. If you are going to do what it is that I do, being a rancher, well, you can't lay down and roll over.

On the front page of The New Mexican *in the spring of* 1979 *there was this surprising headline:*

THE WEST, U.S., LOCKED IN 'WAR'

And the story began: "There's a quiet little war going on out here in the West. There are no trenches, no troops, no tanks. In fact, that's why few people know about this war. . . . And the combatants? On one side are the overregulated, underpopulated —but resource rich—Western states. On the other side: The United States Government and thousands of federal bureaucrats."

That "war" that The New Mexican *reported had been discovered by a "foreign correspondent" from* The New York Times, *earlier that spring. He had toured the "battlefields" and he found that no section of the nation felt as "alienated" as did the West.*

But these newspapers were reporting the wrong "war." They had not asked the ranchers.

If there was a "war" it was not between the western states and the federal government. Most state officials had, however reluctantly, long since acquiesced to urban plans to strip-mine the West of its rural energy resources.

The conflict was more serious than a newspaper "war." It was a struggle for the survival of the western way of life, between urban and rural needs, between agriculture and industry, between the cities and the countryside, between energy producers and energy consumers, between the East and the West.

And the modest, laconic, soft-spoken, lay-back ranchers had become the frontline soldiers in that "war." They seemed an unlikely army.

In the range wars of old the ranchers had done well enough. But they were not equal to the huge energy-consuming corporations. They did not understand corporate ways. One survey of hundreds of ranchers, in the Montana/Wyoming high plains, reported that the ranchers were hurt and surprised that some corporations seemed "deceitful and interested solely in making money." That wasn't very neighborly.

Still, many of the ranchers decided to hold onto their land. And fight.

The image of that small, white-haired woman rancher, Ellen Cotton, riding her fences with an imaginary rifle, and standing guard on her corrals, is one that will not leave my mind. She would do it too. I have no doubt of that.

For miles around her remote ranch the earth had been disemboweled. Some of the largest coal strip mines in the world were within a few hours' ride, by horseback, from her front porch. And yet, if they were to strip-mine up to her front gate, she would undoubtedly refuse to budge an inch.

She did have a rifle.

A Gun in Each Hand, to Stop the Bastards
Ellen Cotton

Some old boy came out here. And I thought he was a feed salesman. I saw him strutting by the corral.

And he said, Do you want to lease your land for coal?

And I said, Hell, no!

And he said, Would you like to sell your place for good money?

And I said, Christ, no!

And he said, If they offered you enough money, wouldn't you sell?

And I said, This land means more to me than all the coal in the world. I love this land. Besides, money won't do me any good on this ranch. What could I do with money?

And he kept on and on and on.

Finally, I said, By God! I don't know what's going to happen. But, by God! I may have to stand with a gun, a gun in each hand to stop you bastards.

And then he departed in haste.

This place is nothing. It is so small. And I'm a small rancher. But it symbolizes something to me, something I would die for.

Money just isn't the thing in my life. That's not why I ranch.

No rancher is in ranching just for the money; if he was he'd be in another business. If you wanted to make money on this place you'd have to be a hard-nosed person. And we'd have no room for anything else, the dollar sign would be your God.

That's not for me. I suppose that I could do it, if I had to, but that's not for me.

Sometimes I go to Denver, or Billings, and I get up on the hills, there, and see all this magnificent agricultural land being chopped up. My God!

For what?

These hideous housing developments. These hideous shopping centers. If they were building beautiful things it wouldn't be so bad. But they are building hideous and horrible housing that people can't be comfortable and happy living in. They look so impersonal. So inhuman. No wonder that tornadoes like to come and to destroy those things.

And that's what all this coal mining will be. It will destroy us.

Coal is a one-crop deal. They are making a sincere effort to revegetate those strip-mined lands, which is not easy, because even where the homesteaders plowed up the land, in those old days, there are still big scars all around us. And the native grasses just don't come back. And then there is the water. People think the water is the easiest thing to have. Even in this country, which is pretty well watered, if they go on strip-mining they don't really know if they are spoiling our water supply. Even in the country, water is pretty desolate.

Oh, I just love this whole country so much. Just the way it sets. It's more valuable than any coal they can take out of it, or any development they can put on it. And it will be forever more valuable to our country, as it is.

And it's just that people who are on the land, like people at sea, they get in touch with natural forces. By gosh! By gosh! The people in urban areas, they don't have that anymore. They don't depend on the weather. They don't need to see the stars.

When you deal with natural forces of weather and wind it keeps you in your place. And you don't think you're too big, in any direction, because it keeps you set down on the earth.

The land that we have, we ought to not let it get too torn

up and destroyed and developed. And turned into something it wasn't meant to be. As for this land, out here, that was settled up about last of any in the United States, this land is worth more in natural grass which is of a very high quality, than all the coal they can get out of it.

Any country that disregards its agriculture didn't last very long. That is something we have to pay attention to. I think our rural way of life is the foundation of this country. Because the people who live on the land learn to respect it, and to survive. Not fighting against the natural forces, but learning to live with them.

It seems to me that when you are living with natural forces that are all around you, you get a concept, a bigger feeling of what is important, a greater concept of things just beyond material values. Not in complete harmony with the forces of nature, but on terms with the forces.

Ranch life is terribly important to hold onto. Our country is getting to be so urbanized that rural people they don't matter much anymore. But they do. The real soul of America is in its land and people close to the land.

And that's why I just can't give up my land.

"With the buffalo already gone, the antelope, which soon will be only a memory, is passing the virile type of man who blazed the trail west," lamented the turn-of-the-century rancher and cowpuncher, R. W. (Bert) Sears, in his Cycle of the Sod. *Of his fellow old-timers, Sears said, "Their autobiography may serve as their obituary." And rather than sorrow, he set forth across four continents to "search for an open range country comparable to that of our old west."*

He did not find it. It "does not exist," he said.

All that was written nearly half a century ago. Though it could just as well have been written one hundred years before that, or today.

For generations the perennial lament of the cowboy and cowman has been that the Old West, the real West, was dead. It died, they said, when the first plow dug up the buffalo grass and the first barbed wires fenced the open range. And it died every year, ever since.

No old-timer who ever lived could not tell you exactly when death occurred. He knew it because he dated it from his lost youth, the passing of his innocence. The westerner, Thoreau had said, was "Adam in Paradise," and he had been exiled from his Garden by the laws of modern life and the blasphemous snake of progress.

Biblical words somehow seemed to fit the rancher's travail. There was an elemental tone to his lament and the curse that was upon him.

The Skinner family of Jordan Valley liked to think of themselves as practical people. And they were. But they had that biblical affinity in them.

On a fifth-generation ranch no one could live apart from the memory of the ecstasy of Jeremiah and the pain of Job, of one's family. The memory of the past was everywhere; it was in the old, fallen building of the original homestead; it was in the weathered barns and corrals; it was in the earth beneath one's feet where the bones of past generations lay.

And so, in spite of himself, when a rancher like Robert Skinner talked about what he called "hard facts" of his life, his words touched the eternal verities of the spirit.

The End of the Trail
Robert Skinner, Sr.

And suppose'n I die. And we have to dig up more money than we have to pay for my inheritance taxes. Then the place has to be sold. That's the cold 'n' hard facts, it appears to me that's closing in on us. Lot of the ranches in our valley have given up because of that. There are very few in the original hands. Now, the way things are going, the chances of my children getting fixed and going on with ranching get slimmer and slimmer all the time.

My son here, trying to live within the framework of the inheritance law that they've set down for us, well, we're having a terrible time trying to get him legally involved to inherit our own ranch. He's here. He's working and all. But it's just very tough turning this ranch over every generation, like you have to, and to keep it in the family.

Why?

Because of the taxes on it and the high value they put on the land. The land values are appreciating wildly. But that don't help the rancher any. It just makes it harder to pay taxes on it.

The big corporations that have the money to invest in the land, why, they can continue ranching. We can't. We don't have that backlog of money. So it's the folks from the cities who are buying up our ranch land. And that causes the land prices to go up even more.

A rancher can't eat the added value to the land. Unless he sells out.

But the demand for the land is not for agricultural production. And that's why these land sales are so out of whack. They want the land to build houses on and to build roads, for city folks, that takes the land out of production. And they want the choice land; the road has to go where it's easiest, so it goes through the valley bottom where the best meadows and pastures are.

So that doesn't do us a bit of good. It does not increase agricultural production. It doesn't help us in any way. It is just a way of putting us out of the ranching business.

Is that what the country wants? Is that what the government wants?

Now, everybody knows we got to have some government, though I think we got too much. And we will pay our fair shares of the taxes. But if you want to preserve our way of life, then you got to fix some way for succeeding generations to take over a ranch, when the older ones pass away. And if you really want to preserve the family farm and ranch, there has got to be a way for our sons and daughters to go on here for another generation.

And we think that's important. Not just to us. To the whole country. On this ranch we think that raising food is important; that if this ranch goes there will be one less place to produce beef for the table. I don't think the people in New York City think that way at all. They think if this ranch goes, so what! There will be another one spring up to take our place. But that's not so.

Our ranching way of life is disappearing fast. Very fast.

If my son can't take over the way I did, then we can go on only so far down the road and then we are done. And I am afraid that our way of life, if that's what you call it, will come to a screeching halt. Whether we like it or whether we don't, whether we fight it or whether we don't, a man can only go on in ranching until he is at the end of his financial ability. Whether you want to or not you still have to look at that damn dollar. And when we can't even pay the taxes on land prices we didn't cause to go up, then we can't go ahead.

Since my great-grandfather came to this country, here, the ranch has been our only source of income. Our only work. If we can't continue doing that and making a living then we've reached the end of the trail. And our way of life is gone. Not only our way of life, but our way of making our way of life.

My family has been here a hundred years. And I don't want to be the one to throw in the sponge. So, I will stay on the ranch until the end. I won't give in so easy. No, I won't.

And my son feels the same way.

The Epilogue

10

The old man gave me his hand. It was streaked with his pale, watery blood that ran down the back of his hand, between his knuckles, and on to my hand, and he held my hand lovingly in that tight grip of his and would not let go until our handclasp was sealed with his blood in a brotherly grasp. On his jaw there was an open cancer, like a gunshot wound, that was dripping blood on his hand and down his neck and across his chest.

My fingertips were red with his blood. It was sticky.

And he looked at me with sorrowful eyes and smiled faintly. "It's good to see you," he said. His eyes said, for one last time.

"It has been a long time," I said, "since we visited."

"That was a better time," he said.

"Boyd, you're a tough old bastard," I said. "You know that."

"Nowadays, I'm good for nothing," he muttered in disgust.

Sadly, he turned his helpless eyes, now dulled with pain and morphine, toward me and he nearly wept. "I hope you never get into the shape I am in," he said. As if it was a personal insult, his illness angered him; he was embarrassed by the indignity of it. And suddenly there was a flash of fury in his eyes that I recognized, that querulous look, when he squinted, that could nail a man to the wall, at fifty paces.

Once, a few years ago, I had described him in this way:

"Old Boyd Charter was ornery. He was one of the last of the

old-time ranchers, who owned his own place on earth and knew his own mind. He was one of those men who are so independent they seem unreal, but he was real enough. The sort of wiry, resilient, honest, straight-faced, outspoken, tough, boyishly polite and shy man who made the West what it once was.

"He was the breed of man who always seemed to have a four-day-old growth of beard.

"Some would call him a relic of the impossible past, conservative as hell, his ideas as hard as nails, his face lined as an old leather saddle, the breeder of rodeo horses and American dreams, with vinegar on his tongue and flint in his eyes."

Even now, with cancer eating up the right side of his face, he hadn't changed all that much. His temperament was just as ornery as ever.

His bedroom where he lay supposedly dying was just off the ranch sitting room. But you could not visit him while he lay in bed. He would not stand for that, being seen in bed, like a sick man. A visitor had to wait until he got out of bed and walked into the sitting room, where he would sit in an upright chair, as he did now, straight as he could, to receive his guest with the proper dignity.

The cancer was nothing new to him. He had it on his lip some years ago. And the doctors thought then they had stopped its growth; they were wrong.

In the spring it had begun to act up again, this time in his jaw. Boyd went to see the doctors who wanted to operate, but they said they couldn't guarantee anything, any hope or any cure.

"Well, I know that!" Boyd thundered, and he walked out of the hospital. He was damned if he would let the doctors cut him up just so they could practice their profession on him.

And so, he went home to his ranch in the Bull Mountains of Montana. There, that summer, he was surrounded by his loving family and the beloved tall grasses of his rangeland. If he had to die he was going to do it, as he had done everything all his life, in his own way.

The grass was silently blowing in the breeze. On his ranch the old buffalo grass was tall as it had been a hundred years ago, before the white man had come; he was proud of that. Some of the movie *Little Big Man* had been filmed on his rangeland because the grassy hills were so high and wild; he was proud of that, too, being able to walk in grass that was not knee high, but was high as a "woman's breasts."

Sitting there, in his ranch house, after a Sunday afternoon steak barbecue, of one of his grass-fed cows, the whole family had gathered. His daughter-in-law said in a way as if to comfort him, "The grass is real tall this summer. It hasn't been this tall in years."

Boyd looked at her, uncomprehending, his mind wandering.

"The grass is near shoulder high," his son said. "Dad, it's real good grass this summer."

And Boyd now nodded. I sat beside him and the left side of his face, which was untouched by the cancer, seemed alive and sharp as it had ever been. The right side of his face kept bleeding.

"Good," he smiled, and he wiped the blood from his cancerous jaw.

Earlier that summer I had written to say I wished to come to visit, to talk about the old days for this book. "That's all he talks about these days," his wife, Anne, had replied. "But you better hurry. He's pretty weak." And yet, I was uneasy about visiting with a man on his deathbed. So I telephoned to say maybe I better not come. His wife said simply, "He's expecting you."

"He always was a tough so and so," I had said.

"Still is," she replied.

Boyd Charter was a living legend, twice over. In the beginning he was known as the son of the man who ran the horses for Butch Cassidy and the Hole-in-the-Wall gang; his father had ridden into history with Cassidy and the Sundance Kid. He remembered, as a boy, his family had settled in country so untamed and virgin that it was "just as the Indians had left it," he said; "no one had time to ruin it." They had to ride their wagons through the rivers, because there were no trails. Later, as he grew up, he became a cowboy, horse wrangler, corraler of wild horses and rancher in his own right, but he was still thought of as the son of his father. It was the outlaw blood in his veins, people said, that made him ornery.

And then he became a legend in his own time. It happened like this: The Government and corporate officials had discovered what they called the energy crisis. To unearth the energy needed for the cities they decided it was necessary to strip-mine the coal of the West. And the coal deposits beneath the buffalo grass on Boyd's ranch were said to be fabulous. He refused to let them dig. He would not sign any coal leases. He politely threw them off his land.

Some people said his personal orneriness was obstructing progress. Some people said he was living in the twentieth century, but his mind was in the nineteenth century. Some people said he was nothing but a relic of the past who ought to be put in a museum case. They may all have been right. Probably they were. But to Boyd he was merely defending a way of life and a way of thinking, the only ways he knew, the ways of a rancher.

Before he knew what had happened, he had become a symbol; both a hero and a villain. There were times when he may have felt much as his father had during his outlaw years.

On that summer afternoon it became so hot that the mosquitoes and horseflies were mean-tempered with the heat. And so, when Boyd had gone back to bed, we sat in the kitchen of the ranch house, seeking a bit of shade. Since Boyd had such difficulty in talking, his words choking in his inflamed throat, Anne asked me if I would like to hear a song about his obstinate doings. It was written by a farmer on the plains of eastern Montana, Charlie Yaeger, and was dedicated to her husband's refusal to lease or sell any of their land to the coal companies to strip-mine the millions of tons of coal beneath it.

The song was sung by Bob Yaeger, Charlie's father. He had a voice like an old needle on a Victrola phonograph; it just scratched along. And the words went something like this:

> In my life I have written myself
> a song or two,
> Songs about the good times, times

of bein' blue,
Songs about the strip mines, tearin'
    up the land,
But never one about the man who led
    the final stand.

This ain't a song about a man whose
    life is steeped in wealth and fame,
Just a song about a man's life whose
    like we'll never see again.
His daddy rode with Cassidy, when he
    was just fourteen,
And that outlaw's love of freedom flows
    freely through his veins.

You're one of a kind, Boyd,
You're the last of a breed.

You're the kind of man
It's gonna take
To keep America free.

You're the kind of man
I thought had died
A long, long time ago.

The kind of man who'd
Never for paper gold
Sell his mortal soul.

Consolidated Coal came to the Bulls
    one day,
They said, Mister Charter, we've a deal
    you know we're gonna make,
We're so rich and powerful, we know,
    you just can't refuse,
The name is on the bottom line; the
    dollars are up to you.

Boyd turned to Anne and his eyes
    fought back the tears,

He thought of all the good times,
      the hardships through the years,
And he said, I can't sell the sky to you,
      boy, for it don't belong to me,
My heritage is not for sale,
      nor are my children's dreams.

Our backs are against the wall now;
      there's no place left to hide,
The West is going to stand and fight
      and maybe some will die,
But our dyin' ain't the hardest thing
      you're ever gonna see,
'Cause when we die, America dies, but
      by God, we're gonna die free.

Boyd, you are the kind of man
      I'd like my kids to meet;
They're not old enough to realize
      What you done for them and me;
So, I'll just take the time to thank
      you in the best way I can;

In years to come, I know
      they'll all understand.

On his deathbed, on his bloodstained sheets, Boyd stirred when he heard the song. He sat up. He listened to his life and I imagine he smiled.

He was too ornery to die easily. He did not know how.

And yet, just three weeks after our last talk together, on Saturday, the twenty-sixth of August, 1978, death came to Boyd Charter. His ashes were scattered in the tall grass of his ranch.

Some years ago, in his own words, he had offered me his own obituary:

"I say we have to stand still. And fight to preserve America. We have no choice, at all. We have our backs against the wall. We are going to be the last generation of western men if we lose. There's no place to pioneer anymore. Nowhere to go. Nowhere to run to. Nowhere to hide.

"When we die, America dies."

So, Boyd, may I dedicate this book to you. It seems the proper thing to do. Even though I know if you were here you'd curse me for doing so immodest a thing.

A Note About the Author

Born in New York in 1925, Stan Steiner now lives in Santa Fe, New Mexico. He is the author and editor of more than a dozen books, many of which explore the history and cultural diversity of America.

A NOTE ON THE TYPE

This book was set in Linotype in a modern adaptation of a type designed by the first William Caslon (1692–1766), greatest of English letter founders. The Caslon face, an artistic, easily read type, has had two centuries of ever increasing popularity in our own country—it is of interest to note that the first copies of the Declaration of Independence and the first paper currency distributed to the citizens of the newborn nation were printed in this type face.

Book composed by American–Stratford Graphic Services, Inc. and printed and bound by The Maple Press Company, York, Pennsylvania.

Book Design by
Albert Chiang